Mark Vernon is an Honorary Research Fellow in Philosophy at Birkbeck College, London. He is a journalist and the author of *The Philosophy of Friendship*, *After Atheism: Science, Religion and the Meaning of Life* and *42: Deep Thought, on Life, the Universe and Everything*. He lives in South London. Visit his website at www.philosophyandlife.com.

What Not to Say

Philosophy for Life's Tricky Moments

MARK VERNON

PHOENIX

A PHOENIX PAPERBACK

First published in Great Britain in 2007
by Weidenfeld & Nicolson
This paperback edition published in 2008
by Phoenix,
an imprint of Orion Books Ltd,
Orion House, 5 Upper St Martin's Lane,
London WC2H 9EA

An Hachette UK company

10 9 8 7 6 5 4 3

ISBN 978-0-7538-2432-0

Typeset at The Spartan Press Ltd,
Lymington, Hants

Printed in Great Britain by Clays Ltd, St Ives plc

The Orion Publishing Group's policy is to use papers that
are natural, renewable and recyclable products and
made from wood grown in sustainable forests. The logging
and manufacturing processes are expected to conform to
the environmental regulations of the country of origin.

www.orionbooks.co.uk

This book is in memory of Joan Barham

Contents

Acknowledgements

Very special thanks to Catherine Clarke, Alan Samson, Matthew Harrison, Nick George.

Introduction

Everyone has them. 'I didn't know what to say!' Times when you are silenced – overwhelmed with embarrassment, gobsmacked, dumbstruck – because someone confronts you with a situation, and you have no idea how to respond. It may be a friend, a colleague or a stranger. You may be at work, in the pub or under the duvet. It may be a matter of love or death, a question of honesty or belief. And the worst thing is – you then say the wrong thing.

What Not to Say takes those situations, unpacks them with philosophy and, understanding gained, explores what is at stake.

Why philosophy? Because philosophy has always been about the questions of life. It was Socrates who first raised the question of how to live. He launched a tradition that stretches from then until now. It sees life not as a problem to be solved, but as an art. It majors on what might be called 'empathy with intelligence'. It also understands that the moments when we are stunned or confounded – lost for words – are some of the most valuable in life. It is then that people find themselves at the limits of their understanding, and may be ready to appreciate more.

What Not to Say can also be thought of as an exercise in

ethics or applied philosophy. This recognises that for the ancient Greek and Roman philosophers the 'how to live' question was just as important as the question that has arguably come to dominate modern philosophy, that is the question of 'how to know'. Thought was therapy. Ancient philosophers routinely posed pressing questions about various predicaments, and sought practical answers.

Coupled to this are the insights of existential philosophy. This asks what it is to experience, to live and to die. It illuminates the anxieties that confuse us when we are wondering what to say to people facing serious life situations.

What Not to Say might therefore be said to have three broad aims. First, to enable readers to speak more truthfully in difficult circumstances: as the Delphic inscription had it, to know thyself. Second, to allow readers to talk about personal problems in a wider perspective, something that in itself often eases the pain. Third, to gain an alternative introduction to some of the themes of philosophy, and some of the thoughts of its biggest thinkers.

In short, it is an aid in the search for the wise thing to say, that vital precursor to the wise way to live.

Forging friendship

'The desire for friendship comes quickly. Friendship does not.'

Aristotle

What can be said

We live in an age of amity. At work, in the gym, through gossip, at the pub, in soaps and, perhaps most emblematically for the networked generation, online. Friendship is apparently all around us.

And yet, friendship – and forging new friendships in particular – can be a great source of anxiety. People without friends at work are twelve times less likely to find their employment satisfying, according to recent research. Little wonder that we long for conspiratorial alliances in the office. And this raises another point of tension: trust. If another piece of research is right, people today have plenty of casual acquaintances but fewer close companions along the way.

Then there are the sorts of friendship that seem to be always a little dicey. What of friendship between men and women, and the problem of inter-sexual *frisson*? Or is

3

friendship possible with the boss, between races, or amongst citizens who radically disagree?

You see, with the best will in the world, there is a huge gap between being friendly and being a friend. That difference can be confused, leading to unfortunate misunderstandings and inappropriate things being said. Someone may ask a favour that is a favour too far, or presume and presume too much. Another may ask for candid advice, though you think that if you gave it the friendship could not bear it. Occasionally, a friend will say 'I love you'. Does your heart sink, not sing?

I have a friend called, let us say, Holly who told me about a friendship she had with a man called, say, Noah. They met at work and an office comradeship flourished; they sent emails, did lunch, and muttered against their bosses. So when he moved jobs it seemed natural to stay in touch. The problem was how. Mere emails did not seem enough.

A drink after work was not practical. So, Holly thought, why not choose an evening and meet up for dinner?

The trouble was that, even as she thought it, Holly became conscious of a snag: the question of sex. At one level, this was ridiculous. Holly is happily married, and shows it, and although Noah was single at the time, the relationship was comfortably, immovably platonic.

But still, going out for dinner seemed inappropriate. It felt like the sort of thing lovers do, not friends. Worse, for all that Holly thought she should resist the thought and just have the dinner, she could not. Indeed, having thought it, the 'non-question' of sex asserted itself as if it were actually a possibility! Like an annoying stain suddenly discovered on a piece of clothing, the relationship came to carry an unwelcome erotic tinge. She never quite managed to shed it.

What is at stake

Aristotle was the first philosopher to define friendship. In his *Nicomachean Ethics* he says that it is 'mutually shared goodwill' – not, on the face of it, a tremendously inspiring definition. But his next step is more profound. It illuminates many of the perils, and possibilities, for amity. He proposes that there are three main types:

Utility friendship. This is the kind that people form as a result of doing something together. The obvious example is work friendship. Initially at least, people become friends at work either because of their shared projects and tasks, or because they have to be together, eight hours a day, five days a week. These friendships offer the huge advantage of giving otherwise rather functional offices or dreary factories a human face. But, in terms of the depth of the affection, they are typically rather fragile. If you take the work away – say, when someone changes job – then these friendships tend to flounder, even when people have worked together for quite some time.

Pleasure friendship. This is the kind people form because of an activity in common that they enjoy and share. It might be shopping or football. The example Aristotle takes is a relationship that is almost purely sexual and based upon the exchange of carnal pleasures. This would lead to a friendship of sorts. But, like utility friendship, if the shared activity ceases – because, say, the sex loses its passion – then the friendship will dissolve too.

These first two types of friendship depend for their

existence on something apart from the friends themselves. This is both their strength, because they come into being relatively quickly, and their weakness, because they often don't go very deep.

Excellent friendship. Aristotle's third, quintessential kind of friendship – what he calls excellent friendship – does not suffer from being dependent upon something else. It is friendship that forms because you love another for whom they are in themselves – for their excellent qualities, character and humanity. It lasts for the very reason that it does not depend upon something external to the friendship but on who and what the friends are as lovely and lovable people. It is driven forward by the desire to get to know each other better and to live life together more fully. It is the friendship of soulmates. It will include things that are done and enjoyed *à deux*, like the friendships of utility and pleasure. But if those things should cease, the friendship would remain.

From this threefold categorisation, many practical insights into friendship follow – insights that have a direct bearing upon what to say, and what not to say, to friends.

What not to say

Deeper friendship takes time to form. Aristotle again: 'The desire for friendship comes quickly. Friendship does not.' So someone who swears undying friendship within hours of meeting; or someone who claims to have hundreds of friends – online or in real life; or someone who declares that they haven't seen their best friend in months, perhaps years, and yet when they do meet they know it will be as if they have never been apart – all these people might be accused of taking friendship for granted. It would certainly not be surprising if the person in whom they placed so much confidence secretly, and eventually in their deeds and words, expressed disquiet with the relationship.

So if when you meet someone and a friendship appears spontaneously to ignite, be glad but be cautious. If you realise you are on someone's list of hundreds of 'fantastic friends', understand the limits of such affection. If you haven't seen your best friend in weeks and weeks, then you might do well to pick up the phone.

A related reflection is that best friends know each other intimately. 'A friend is another self' was Aristotle's formula – capturing two insights about the closest friendships. First, you know a soulmate perhaps better than you know yourself. Second, the true friend is someone for whom you feel and care as much as you care for yourself. But remember that there are three kinds of friendship. Many times when someone with whom you are friendly says something that over-steps the mark – 'invades your space' – what they have done is confuse a lesser kind with the higher. Keeping that in mind can help you to understand and respond accordingly.

Another thing: there is a careful balance to be drawn in friendship between being useful to a friend and feeling used by them. If a reasonably good friend asks you to feed the cat for a couple of days, you may well be only too glad to help. After all, it might deepen the friendship. But if they make the same request for two months, you could feel they are asking too much. Only you can tell. Aristotle offers a guiding principle: 'Friends do not put the scales centre stage.' If you sense the scales are out – that you are being somewhat used – then it might well be best to say 'no' there and then.

What of friendship between men and women? We will deal elsewhere with the case in which sex is explicitly on the cards. For now, what of the case in which sex is not, apparently, on the agenda? Well, here's one marker. If you speak to virtually any relationship expert, they will tell you that such relationships are strewn with erotic pitfalls. These hazards increase in number in direct proportion to the closeness of the relationship. The issue is intimacy, and platonic intimacy becoming confused with physical intimacy.

Incidentally, for Aristotle the problem didn't arise. It was not that he thought men were from Mars and women from Venus. It was that he presumed that women were 'lesser' men, lesser particularly in their rational capabilities. He therefore regarded mixed-gender friendships as inherently limited. In this he was not exceptional, just of his time.

Today, we must, I suppose, take the psychologists seriously. But I think philosophy suggests that the situation is more hopeful than might otherwise be thought. Friendship is an intellectual kind of love – it delights in the soul not the body. This is why the characteristic activity of friends is to talk. It is also why sex and friendship do not, as a rule, mix – the one exception being the unique synthesis of sex and friendship that people hope to achieve with a husband, wife or partner.

If, however, you can say with hand on heart that it is friendship you desire with your acquaintance of the opposite sex, then remember that it will flourish when the heart is led by the head. C. S. Lewis had an illuminating image. Lovers gaze into each other's eyes, he wrote. Friends, together, look straight ahead. If you find the eyes are beckoning, be careful!

One final thought: Shakespeare, along with many others who have thought deeply about friendship, was wary of it. 'Most friendship is feigning,' he argued, although he added: 'most loving mere folly.' If this seems rather cynical, there is a hard truth in it. The ideal of friendship is that nothing separates the parties concerned. 'Friends have all things in common,' Aristotle said. And yet in practice friendship is often a complex, subtle process of negotiation, and working out just how much you should say.

The advice is to choose your moment. Do you really like the new boyfriend? Does he actually look thinner on top? Is her novel in fact bad? Take half a breath. Feigning – waiting for the moment in which the truth can be spoken in honesty *and* in love – is better than blunt words blurted out that sound as brutal as a bludgeon.

Falling in love

'Love is blind.'   Anon

What might be said

The thought is irrepressible: your good friend has fallen for the wrong person, at the wrong time, in the wrong way. You meet the said new boy- or girlfriend, and, even as you hold out your hand, you involuntarily take a step back. What is the attraction? Where is the appeal? For all that you try to be jolly, you are thinking something else. Your friend's infatuation is as mysterious to you as the princess's was for the green frog – and it will take more than a kiss to turn this one into a prince. They are not star-crossed but ill-matched, a voice repeats in your head. And then you have darker thoughts: does he need money, a passport, a flat? Is it her biological clock ticking over like a self-destruct bomb?

Whatever it might be, one thing is clear: the relationship cannot receive your blessing. But you know it must. Your friendship requires it. And, of course, it could be that you are wholly and utterly wrong. Appeasement or compliance would appear to be the best policy.

I once knew a young man. Let's call him Angel, because he was innocent. I liked Angel. It is heart-warming to have a friend who is routinely delighted by life, and you would have thought that love would easily come his way too. He had clear skin, soft features and honey-coloured hair. The worst that could be said against him was a slight loose-jointedness when he walked.

But love was difficult for him. It was as if he could never quite close the deal, for all that he wanted to. Later he confessed to me that when people used to say he was 'so nice' – meaning that he was eligible – he was so irritated that he almost cursed. In retrospect, he wondered whether falling in love with Foxy – we'll call her that because she was wily and manipulative – had been a kind of protest. He almost wanted her to hurt him.

No one knew what to say the day they walked into the pub together, though immediately we knew. Love was stamped on their faces. He looked elated. She looked triumphant. (A friend muttered, 'Devil incarnate!') Yet it was obvious that it would end in tears, her slyness being to his naivety as raw sewage is to fresh water – environmentally damaging. But we were silent, at least when in earshot. What can you say to someone who finds love reciprocated at last?

And after Foxy? Angel didn't fall in love again, at least during the time that I knew him.

What is at stake

Roland Barthes, the French cultural critic who died in 1980, thought life was an experience that is strange, precipitous and without closure, its meaning 'infinitely deferred' – which is a smart way of saying beyond reach. But do not fear. Throw yourself into it, he said, with *jouissance*.

You would have been unwise, therefore, to ask Barthes for financial advice or for a sound legal decision. But he is an excellent guide to the madness that is called love. In his book, *A Lover's Discourse*, he sketched out the terrain by reflecting on the utterances of an imagined individual who is in love. By reminding us what people think when they fall in love, he expands on what is at stake.

For example, actions that seem absurd to those out of love or long in love, are to those newly caught up in love exactly the opposite; they are signs of sanity and strength. Someone who is infatuated will cling to a mobile phone in case it rings, as a baby does to its bottle. Decisions that before would have been made in an instant are now treated with vacillation, as if the lover has been rendered incapable of ever thinking for themselves again. They will understand implicitly what the diva meant when she crooned about not being able to breathe unless her lover was resting beside her.

What is going on here is the joy of dependency, says Barthes. The burden of being responsible is relinquished in happy subjugation to the beloved. The more trivial the distraction – the more abject the humiliation – the more it paradoxically proves the love. The impassioned lover does not want to reason because that would mean becoming responsible again.

Another thing that is striking about new lovers is that they like nothing better than to talk about their love. The signs of it blossoming are here, there and everywhere. Someone who has fallen in love will be delighted to share its endless subtleties with you. But what is happening in their favourite soap, the shenanigans of the office, the pro-gress of their football team – all the old staples of your friendship – suddenly seem dull to them when set against the infinite nuances of their new relationship.

This ditching of interests reveals something important. In fact, says Barthes, what is subtle is not their love but the way they can talk so copiously about it. The talk is a gloss, an unreal interpretation of what has happened that, probably unconsciously, diverts attention from the possibility that the newfound feeling might not deliver on its promise, might not be an answer to life after all. So your intuitions about the inappropriateness of the relationship could well be right – though to suggest as much would seem like pure contempt, as cynical as signing a prenuptial agreement on the morning of a marriage.

New lovers may go so far as to say that they love their beloved more than they love their own life. They are caught up in a kind of amorous catastrophe, an emotional runaway train – elated by the speed, fearless of any crash. They would prefer to despair of life itself than to turn away from the love that has apparently breathed life into them with a force they never thought possible. 'I have projected myself into the other with such power that when I am without the other I cannot recover myself, regain myself: I am lost, for ever,' Barthes wrote. It is the Romeo and Juliet syndrome; poison's embrace is preferable to no embrace.

What not to say

What this adds up to is that your friend has refused the thought that love can be blind. Moreover, they insist that it is exactly the opposite. Love has opened their eyes. It is leading them into all truth. It is only by being with their beloved that they can be themselves. This is what puts you in an impossible position: to offer even the gentlest critique of the lover is not only to risk upsetting your friend; it is to become a blasphemer – a denier of the truth. The risk is that they will then become angry. They will accuse you of lying out of fear that you will lose them. Or perhaps, they may suggest, you are jealous and want the beloved for yourself.

You cannot reason with them. They think they know more about love than you possibly can. Even if they were minded to add up all the pluses and minuses, and countenance the negatives outweighing the positives, they would say that that misses the point. Like belief in God, love is beyond probabilities. Calculation is evaporation. And anyway, love will mend him; it will change her.

There is, however, one thing that you could try. In a word, friendship – deployed in two ways.

First, reply that you look forward to getting to know the new boyfriend or girlfriend better, to becoming their friend too. This is partly a delaying tactic, since befriending someone takes time and so excuses you from the immediate need to pass judgement. It also suggests a process, defusing the impetuous tyranny that love can be. 'Love's not time's fool,' Shakespeare mused, celebrating the love that does not change with time and forgetting, at least in Sonnet 116, the love that despises time for the fool that the months and years can make of it.

Second, encourage your friend to themselves befriend their beloved, to get to know them better too. This sounds positive and is easy for them to do, since any excuse to spend time together is a good excuse as far as they are concerned. However, there is method in this apparent magnanimity. One of the reasons that love is blind is that it can happen so quickly, with little self-disclosure. Desire clouds vision – which is why the beloved looks flawless in the eyes of the lover. Real friendship, though, can dispel the swirls of emotion, and reveal what is truly lovely, and what is not. Take heart. Your friend may come to see the faults you so quickly spotted in their new lover for themselves.

Wanting sex

'Nobody dies from lack of sex. It's lack of love we die from.'

Margaret Atwood

What might be said

You could be forgiven for thinking that no one refuses sex any more. It is, apparently, as easy to come by as a Coke, and probably less shaming to indulge in. Evolutionary psychologists tell us that we are driven by our genes, whose whole purpose is to propagate; it is surprising our towns and cities do not come to a halt, given all the grinding our raw biology would apparently have us do. Screens – TV, billboard and computer – offer a 24/7 parade of beautiful bodies to lure us. It is sometimes said that in the urban jungle you are never more than a few feet away from a rat. Whatever the truth of that, you are never more than a few seconds away from soft curves and firm pecs.

Of course, people do want sex, but mostly not just any sex. There are the times when the sex would not be consensual, and that can be condemned *tout à fait*. But assuming we are considering a level playing-field, I suspect that nine times out of ten, if asked, people might prefer to decline the kind offer. 'No, I do have a headache.' 'Have you looked in the mirror recently?' 'The photocopier is uncomfortable.' 'Beery breath is not charming.' 'But we're friends!' So – just for the sake of argument – let us imagine a time when you do not keep these thoughts to yourself but put your hand up, stand up and say 'no'.

'Hollywood is a place where they'll pay you a thousand dollars for a kiss and fifty cents for your soul,' complained Marilyn Monroe. But sometimes in a Hollywood movie, the lead and the love interest do not end up in bed. When they don't – when the Bond girl does not collapse whimpering, 'Oh James!' – the effect can be striking.

In *Lost in Translation*, directed by Sofia Coppola, Bob, played by Bill Murray, ends up knocking about with – but not knocking up – Charlotte, played by Scarlett Johansson. They meet in a Tokyo hotel, both with time on their hands. Bob is famous and has been flown to Japan, no expenses spared, to feature in a drinks ad; but the shoot is short compared with the length of stay. Charlotte is similarly at a loose end, having come with her husband who has business to attend to. They meet, and flirt and hang out, and end up in the same hotel suite. But the story of their encounter is one that does not result in sex, though it easily could have done so.

Why not? There is a sense that, although an erotic charge hovers between them, to have let it flow would have been to lose something. If they had just slept with each other they would have found release but no real resolution to the problems in the other parts of their lives. Instead, their passion is redirected. They turn it away from each other and towards their separate lives – the lives they must pick up when they part. Which, the film suggests, is what the non-consummation of their encounter enables them to do.

What is at stake

The nineteenth-century philosopher Arthur Schopenhauer is arguably the most innovative modern thinker on sex. He articulated the idea of unconscious drives and repression before Freud, and offered an evolutionary 'explanation' of male promiscuity and female fidelity before Darwin. And all with – or perhaps because of – a persistently unsuccessful sex life.

Just why he had no difficulty with 'no' becomes clearer after reading his parable of the porcupines:

> On a cold winter day, a group of porcupines huddled together closely to save themselves by their mutual warmth from freezing. But soon they felt the stab of their quills and drew apart. And whenever the need for warmth brought them closer together again, this second pain was repeated. They were tossed back and forth between these two kinds of suffering until they discovered a moderate distance that proved the most tolerable.
>
> Thus the need for company, born of the emptiness and monotony inside them, drives people together; but their many revolting qualities and intolerable faults repel them apart again. The medium distance that they finally discover and that makes association possible is politeness and good manners. Whoever does not keep this distance is told, among the British: 'Keep your distance!'
>
> To be sure, this only permits imperfect satisfaction of the need for mutual warmth, but it also keeps one from feeling the prick of the quills.

It is tempting to think that such a world, lacking real

intimacy, would be a sad one. Schopenhauer agrees. For, he continues, there is no such thing as happiness – only the contentment that comes with the absence of pain.

Sexual desire is possibly the best example of this negative state of affairs. Think of the excitement, the thrill, the anticipation, and compare that with the anticlimax afterwards. 'Everyone who is in love will experience an extraordinary disillusionment after the pleasure he finally attains,' Schopenhauer opines. It's like winning the lottery. All the evidence shows that within days, or weeks at most, people return to the low level of discontent that made them buy the ticket in the first place.

The tragedy of the erotic is that it is beyond us to command it. To disagree with Evelyn Waugh, the 'thin bat's squeak of sexuality' is more like a squawk. In fact, according to Schopenhauer, sex is second only in strength to the demonic will that fuels the struggle for animal survival; it lessens only with our last breath. It fills the thoughts of young people even when they are sleeping. It lies behind nearly all the goals for which we strive. It 'intrudes with trash' and 'knows how to slip its love-notes and ringlets even into ministerial portfolios and philosophical manuscripts', Schopenhauer continued. It is the manifest presence of the selfish gene, the 'will to live of the species', that asserts its command even when all our rational powers are lined up against it.

What not to say

And so, for these very reasons, it is good, on occasion, not to acquiesce or stay silent, but to positively refute sex and refuse it. Here are three immediate benefits.

First, it stops you looking ridiculous. Consider again the evolutionary stereotype of the rampant male and nurturing female. Richard Dawkins, in *The Selfish Gene*, accounted for the supposed differences in the sex drives of men and women by arguing that the genes of men are always ready to propagate at the drop of a hat, as it were. Women's genes, on the other hand, are condemned – or is it liberated? – to being able to reproduce only once a month.

Schopenhauer indulged in a similarly laughable speculation when he talked of short men being attracted to tall women, in order that their physical 'disadvantage' would be overcome in their children. And he argued that the 'full female bosom' exerted an 'exceptional charm' because it promised any offspring much nourishment. So, don't make a fool of yourself. Prove sex wrong. Sometimes say no!

Second, and more seriously, Schopenhauer suggests that denial makes something wonderful possible, namely change. If sex is a motor that would ride roughshod over our lives then that does not mean it cannot be suppressed. Suppression is usually thought a bad thing, when unconscious. But when conscious what it makes possible is sublimation and maybe even transformation.

Sublimation occurs when the sexual urge is redirected to immaterial things – the creative juices being turned towards other, non-biological, creative acts. 'Making music is another way of making children,' wrote Nietzsche, a keen student of Schopenhauer. And long before the nineteenth century, Plato had argued that becoming pregnant 'in the soul' might be preferable to becoming pregnant 'in the body', if only because the spiritual offspring of your ideas are yours, unlike your sons and daughters.

Transformation occurs when, as a result of facing your desire, your character changes. It is to examine yourself, something the birds and bees cannot do. Transformation is an almost mystical occurrence for Schopenhauer, since at least in adults, the way we are – our habits, reactions and drives – usually seems fixed. When change happens it seems to have flown in from some transcendent realm. Asceticism is the way to open yourself up to this possibility; denial of the sex drive – on occasion – quintessentially so.

Third, to keep your genes in their place, and tell them you are not a sex machine, is to show that you are a human lover of others, not merely their stud or heifer. To love is to have compassion – that is, to stand apart from your own needs and desires and to put yourself in another's place. For many philosophers, such sympathy is nothing less than a principle of human nature. Evolutionary theory, and its tyranny of lust and procreation, would undo it.

So Schopenhauer, for all his pessimism, fixes a place for sympathy in human life over and above the survival of the fittest. He noted that love and little kindnesses could be seen every day on the streets of Frankfurt, his home town. People are moved by others' suffering, in spite of the irresistibility of their own will. They identify with them and do not pass by on the other side. They feel remorse when someone suffers on their account. To see such empathy in action is to gain an insight into the human condition that is more profound even than sex. It is to see that people are connected, that when one is harmed all are harmed; it is to catch a glimpse of the truth that ultimately everything is a unity.

Which, paradoxically, is also what sex – *loving* sex – gets right, when lovers are conjoined together.

Ending relationships

'Every time I paint a portrait I lose a friend.'   John Singer Sargent

What might be said

It is not only lovers who can become estranged. Friends can too. But whereas lovers end their relationships climactically, in torments and tears, failing friendships can limp on for years – like a grumpy relative who grows older and meaner and forgets to die.

If asked, the friends might admit that the relationship had long lost its savour. Or another person, with a friend clinging like chewing-gum to the bottom of their shoe, would happily confess that they nurse a loathing for them, and yet old habits of association die hard. Others have just changed – though their Christmas card list hasn't. The meaningless expressions of goodwill and affection have gone on for so long they would not now know what else to say. How on earth could they end it?

Friedrich Nietzsche, the philosopher, had few friends. Not because he was 'depressing' or 'misanthropic', as he has been accused of. Rather, he was the sort of person for whom less is more; he chose his friends carefully because he expected much from them, almost as much as he gave.

The trouble is that if you only do high-intensity intimacy, you may live passionately but without the wide circle of long-standing friends that calmer souls enjoy. You are not easy to know. Or to put it another way, you soon become acquainted with the business of ending relationships.

Nietzsche learnt this in an ending of operatic proportions. He met Richard Wagner, the composer, in 1868. Within twelve months he was a close friend, experiencing a plunging affection that revolved around an ecstatic admiration for the maestro's music. In it, Nietzsche found the possibility of transcendence, a depth of feeling of which Wagner, his friend, was the author. Nietzsche, in turn, offered Wagner a philosophy of music that painted him as its most perfect realisation. Neither was given to modesty where greatness was concerned. The friendship was sealed.

Until, that is, the Bayreuth Festival of 1876. Never at home in a herd, Nietzsche was revolted by what he took to be the philistines that crowded in that year to see the opera. Moreover, he suspected that Wagner was compromising himself – dumbing down to build up the takings. He fled the festival with a blinding headache. The split was deep and became permanent.

In fact, at the time, Nietzsche didn't know what to say, and for a while Wagner remained unaware of the rift. Perhaps Nietzsche was shamed by his own inabilities as a composer. Maybe he was repelled by Wagner's deepening religious convictions. Or again, he may have realised that in order to flourish himself he had to leave Wagner's dominating presence, and the only way to do this was with a clean break, like a newborn whose cord must be cut to start life.

Later, though, Nietzsche did find words. They offer a profound reflection on the whys and wherefores of terminating a relationship.

What is at stake

Nietzsche's reflections on the ending of friendship come in his so-called middle period, in books like *Human, All Too Human* and *The Gay Science*. They appeared soon after his split from Wagner. His aphoristic style is to the point and punchy, operating not as sound-bites but as sayings that insist you pause for thought:

'The friend whose hopes one cannot satisfy one would rather have for an enemy.'

'Human relationships rest on the fact that a certain few things are never said, indeed they are never touched upon; and once these pebbles are set rolling, the friendship follows after, and falls apart.'

'If we have greatly transformed ourselves, those friends of ours who have not been transformed become like ghosts of our past; their voice comes across to us like the voice of a shade – as though we were hearing ourself, only younger, more severe, less mature.'

Nietzsche reflected that people who have a gift for friendship tend to fall into two types. The first, he called circle-like. They are the individuals who attract and gather many people around them, their charisma functioning like a bright light that draws creatures in the night. There is a great buzz in knowing such people but, like the champagne they may feed you, much of it is froth and bubbles.

The second group of people who are good at friendship he called ladder-like. For them, life is lived at a stretch. It is a continual process of change and development, and it is their very drive – the sense that they are moving higher – that brings people within their orbit. However, as they scale the rungs, be they professional, artistic or intellectual, they inevitably leave people behind, which if they are at all compassionate can be painful for them.

In short, unlike family, friendship is a relationship of choice: implicit in its logic is the possibility of an end. And sometimes that end is a good choice to make. Indeed, paradoxically, it is only the most profound friendships that may be confronted with that choice. More casual, uncommitted friends will be content merely to drift – sometimes nearby, sometimes further apart, always in a partial state of indifference.

So how can you tell if a friendship is in decline and an attempt should be made at closure? Aristotle suggests a couple of indicators that something is terminally wrong.

First, you may have thought that you knew someone well, and that the basis of the friendship was a genuine love of you for yourself. But then it turns out they were a false friend. They actually only loved the way you made them laugh, and in truth they thought you were a bit of a joke. Or, they sought your company not because of your open character but because of your open wallet. 'Quarrels between friends occur more than anything when there is a difference between what they think the basis of the friendship is and what it actually is,' Aristotle observed. In the case of serious offence, a good ending may be a pipe dream. It could be better to admit the truth of the duplicity and move on.

A second reason for the failure of friendships is that people change. Over the years, a person you once liked might develop ugly flaws. As a lad, he was daring and fun; as a man, he has come to embody the worst excesses of the open market. As a teenager, she was indiscreet and conspiratorial; as a woman she has become embittered and poisonous. What happens here is that the good thing that lay at the foundations of the friendship has crumbled. As a result, a time may come when it is impossible to make the friendship stand up. Honesty now may save a drawn-out process of obfuscation and avoidance later; you can only fake it for so long.

What not to say

Nietzsche was in little doubt that sometimes friendships end. Good beginnings can make for good ends, as the saying goes; if it comes to it, there might be enough goodwill to ease the parting or avoid the need for a direct confrontation. However, sometimes, as with Wagner, it is bound to be messy whatever is said.

Nietzsche conjures up a rather beautiful image. Think of a star in the heavens, he says. Starlight has two characteristics. First, it is bright, even sparkling. Second, it never casts a shadow. Such starlight can stand for a friendship that has had real meaning. Now though, as it has failed, it can be appreciated for what it was. And, most importantly, it doesn't have to cast a shadow over your ongoing life.

Friends are always a gift. And even if at times they bring pain, it is worth making the attempt to remember them gratefully and to think of the old friend graciously.

Marriage and divorce

'Love the quest; marriage the conquest; divorce the inquest.'

Helen Rowland

What might be said

There are few moments more unsettling in life than when your best friend tells you they are engaged to be married. On the surface, all is happiness, joyfulness, celebration. But underneath emerges a fear. Has your friendship now peaked? Will its former closeness be lost, as marriage – the rite that turns two into one – draws your friend from you and into the orbit of another? When they first tell you, of course, you are delighted. But when you think on, you feel anxious, even angry and alone.

Sydney Smith wrote: '[Marriage] resembles a pair of shears, so joined that they cannot be separated; often moving in opposite directions, yet always punishing anyone who comes between them.' This is the worry, though it feels callous to voice it.

The irony is that if marriage can exclude, then it is the same exclusion that makes divorce so difficult for friends too. Sometimes the grounds for divorce are clearly founded – cruelty, infidelity or physical violence being obvious cases. However, more often than not, the reasons for separation are obscure. 'It's just over, I know it,' a friend may tell you. Or: 'For years we have not been in love.' For years! And you had no idea.

It is said that wedlock is a padlock. Well, it is also a screen, behind which silent suffering is readily concealed. It is hard to know what to say when you learn of a divorce, if you have been granted too little access to make an informed judgement.

The outsider status felt by 'sheepish singletons' is brilliantly captured in *Bridget Jones's Diary* by Helen Fielding. Bridget calls married people 'Smug Marrieds'. Dinner parties in their homes reduce her ego to 'the size of a snail'. It is a wholly intimidating experience to be sitting around a table when everyone is coupled, two by two, except you. All that eye contact; all those warm asides that only a partner understands. No man is an island? Rubbish.

They have children, 'plop, plop, plop, left right and centre', Fielding writes – a natal superfluity that seems to be exceeded only by their escalating salaries. United they stand, successful in the world. Single, Bridget Jones withers. They offer their patronising advice to those whose lives aren't as perfect as theirs, i.e. to those who are single. Inevitably, eventually, this involves asking Bridget why she is not married – with the implication of social failure that the question implies echoing across the whole of human history. Her friend Sharon fumes: 'You should have said "I am not married because I am a singleton, you smug, prematurely ageing, narrow-minded morons."'

Smug Marrieds write articles in newspapers for other Smug

Marrieds to read. They go on exotic holidays together. Hell, Smug Marrieds can even be trendy these days, with all the designer goods that are on sale for them!

What is at stake

Plutarch – or Mestrius Plutarchus to give him his full name – was a bit of a prude. He was a Greek author who lived from about 50–125 CE, that is about the same time as St Paul and the other writers of the New Testament were penning the Christian ideals for marriage that shape Western attitudes to this day. His thoughts are remarkably similar, and in terms of their basic morality, were unexceptional for that period. But whereas St Paul's marriage guidance today reads like a series of overbearing proscriptions, Plutarch's more practical suggestions have a lighter feel, one advantage of them never having been taken too seriously in their own time. As such they can be laughed at as freely as they can be learnt from.

Plutarch does have some hilarious pieces of advice. For example, newly weds might consider his advice of eating a quince before retiring to the marriage bed, to ensure that they do not have bad breath. And he argues against the use of music to create a romantic atmosphere, thinking that melodies are best saved for the days in which the bed of roses has become a field of battle.

He is a realist about marriage, notably when it comes to sustaining the passion of the early days. 'Fire takes speedy hold of straw or hare's fur, but soon goes out again, unless fed with an addition of more fuel,' he says. The fuel of marriage is mutual affection, 'enlivened by the intermixture of souls as well as bodies'.

It must be admitted that Plutarch shares the patriarchal prejudices of his Roman confrères. If women should act modestly and submit to their husbands, according to St Paul, Plutarch thinks the same – though unlike St Paul his reason is not theological but aesthetic. There is no more ignominious a sight than a henpecked husband, he declares. To be fair to him, he emphasises the dignity of husband *and* wife, telling Roman husbands that in spite of the notion of *paterfamilias*, that puts them above the law in their own households, they should not be thugs.

I do not know whether Plutarch read the Hebrew Bible, and the myth of Adam and Eve that seems to give divine sanction to Bridget Jones's 'Smug Marrieds', as well as legitimating the conspiracy of two that can make marriage so difficult for close friends. He has his own version of it, however. He notes that the marriage relationship can, in practice, adopt one of several different models. Some couples marry solely because they fancy each other, and, as is the way of the flesh, soon drift apart. Others cleave close for the purpose of having children, but otherwise lead relatively independent lives.

However, the best model for Plutarch is one in which the couple are wholly united, like liquids that mix: 'For as the physicians say that the right side being bruised or beaten communicates its pain to the left; so indeed the husband ought to sympathise in the sorrows and afflictions of the woman, and much more does it become the wife to be sensible of the miseries and calamities of the husband; to the intent that, as knots are made fast by knitting the bows of a thread one within another, so the ligaments of conjugal society may be strengthened by the mutual interchange of kindness and affection.' Indeed, so closely bound should this conjugal society be, that partners ought not to have friends they do not share in their marriage. If they do, then Plutarch believes this will only cultivate habits of secrecy, and that way lies deception.

Well, in a way, that is exactly what the ostracised friend wants. They do not want to be in the marriage, for then it gets crowded. They want a separate relationship, with its own intimacies and secrets, that runs alongside the marriage. This is what is so challenging to the traditional model of marriage with its bonded two.

In fact, external friends need not be the enemy of matrimony but might actually be its saviour. Just why is revealed in Plutarch's discussion of divorce. He tells the story of a certain gentleman who separated from his wife, though she was sober, beautiful, chaste and rich. His friends could not understand why. Until he put forth his foot and showed them his sandal. 'This shoe looks new, elegant and perfectly fitting to you,' he said. 'So you do not know that it pinches me.'

The hidden nature of the rows and disagreements that erode a marriage are exactly what makes them so dangerous. They are like fevers that have no visible cause, and confound the doctors that treat them. 'If daily continued, the petty snubs and frumps between man and wife, though perhaps unknown to others, are of that force that above all things else they canker conjugal affection, and destroy the pleasure of cohabitation,' Plutarch concludes.

What not to say

So, for all that the friend is right to fear being sidelined as a result of the romance of marriage, and for all that they may be tempted to declare, 'It serves you right,' when the couple's relationship subsequently splits apart, they must resist the temptation.

Marriage can be unsettling to those whom it isolates. And divorce can feel like an amputation: as Margaret Atwood described it, 'You survive, but there's less of you.' But it is not good for man to be alone, as the Bible has it. And the friend can play a wonderful part in that, one that in time can again sustain their own need for togetherness, when the newly weds have achieved a balance in their relationship.

What friends can perhaps do in the early days is to initiate the right direction of travel, and borrow some words from *The Prophet*. Even better, suggest them for the wedding. Kahlil Gibran writes:

> *Let there be spaces in your togetherness,*
> *And let the winds of the heavens dance between you.*

The thought has the genius of sounding thoroughly romantic, whilst being sober and wise at the same time. It creates a vital space for extra-marital friendship.

Coping with families

'The awe and dread with which the untutored savage contemplates
his mother-in-law are amongst the most familiar facts of anthropo-
logy.'   James George Frazer

What might be said

The first time you own up about the trials and tribulations
of your family life will not be your last. What a relief! For
years, you may have carried the secret of its pain. As an
adult, it felt too childish to blame your parents; as a parent, it
felt like an admission of failure to blame your child. Each
unhappy family is not only unhappy in its own way but in its
own *secret* way, we might say, adding to Tolstoy's famous
opening line.

However, this silence is a big part of why the sins of the
fathers, and the sorrows of the mothers, are carried down
the generations. Each person who does not talk – in an effort
to talk them out (not merely deepen and repeat them) –
transmits the faults and misery quite as surely as they
transmit their genes.

It is hard to talk, however, because the modern family is

sacrosanct. So much has been loaded onto it that to admit failure in this part of life feels like admitting to the failure of our society as a whole. That may or may not be the case, but one thing is for sure: it is impossible for humans to flourish while families maintain their conspiracies of silence.

At the level of political discourse, the strident repetition of platitudes about the family must count as one of the most vacuous forms of rhetoric invented. I would love to know what 'family values' are, if the term refers to anything other than a motherhood-and-apple-pie decency that no one could question, or the puritanical demonisation of minorities to maintain the Moral Majority's delusion of its flawless home life.

In the UK, a similarly empty phrase has become politically *de rigueur*, namely 'hard-working families'. Again, it is entirely unclear to what or whom this refers. Is it supposed to point a finger of blame at lazy families, whatever their sin may be? What about hard-working bachelors or widows? It is a way of talking about the family that is not talking about real families at all.

Then there is the phrase 'the traditional family'. Again there is no such thing. The 'nuclear family' is a social unit of recent invention: it arose in the West during the nineteenth century when middle-class parents gained the wealth to afford a semi in which to raise the kids. Families before, and elsewhere, know of no such definitional boundaries. Indeed, there is evidence that the invention of the nuclear family was a bad move, as many such clans seem barely able to cope with the strains of modern life. Something approaching half of marriages end in divorce.

And then there is the supposition that the family is the supreme expression of religious virtue. Christians may be surprised to learn that, according to *Cruden's Concordance*, the word 'family' appears only once in the New Testament, and refers then to the family of humankind. If you search for positive endorsements in the Gospels, via Jesus's comments on mothers, brothers and sisters, you will be hard pushed too. Similarly, in the Old Testament, the most notable families are often the most dysfunctional, like that of King David. The ones that work, like those of Ruth and Naomi, are hardly conventional.

What is at stake

For the individual, the challenge of a family is threefold. First, there is no escaping family. Even if, by some horrible accident, a single child's father were to die during the pregnancy and its mother during the birth, that child still has a family, the absent family of the orphan. Second, as in the midst of life we are in death, so it seems that in the midst of family we are in conflict. Whether or not you can sign up to Freud's Oedipus complex in all its details, its broad thrust is surely right. Third, a person's happiness in life has much to do with finding happiness in relation to their family, especially if that is a question of becoming reconciled to a profoundly unhappy one.

In the *Symposium*, Plato's dialogue on *eros* at an ancient Athenian dinner-party, there is one character who stands out as having much to cope with when it came to his family. He was unfortunate enough to have a great and celebrated adoptive father. He was even more unfortunate to be almost, but not quite, a great man himself. It seems that he made the strategic mistake of trying to imitate his father in order to keep the family name alive. The effort infantilised him and was his undoing.

That individual was Alcibiades, the politician, general and – at the time – the most celebrated of the students of Socrates. His adoptive father was Pericles, the man who led Athens in the period that became known as its Golden Age. Pericles ran Athenian policy during the early years of the Peloponnesian War, the city's lengthy conflict with Sparta. When Pericles died, Alcibiades worked his way to the head of the democratic party in his late father's place.

At first, Alcibiades' military brilliance and personal charm suggested that he might outshine his father. However, his need to do so led him into further, unnecessary, wars that turned out to be disastrous. His compatriots turned against him and, despairing that he would ever lead an army again, he deserted to the enemy, the Spartans. It was not a successful move, and a few years later he switched sides again. However, he failed Athens a second time. Exiled, he was subsequently murdered.

Plato set the *Symposium* in 416 BCE, the year before Alcibiades' first and determinate fall; the seeds of his undoing had sprouted. Plato shows this in the profound antagonism that Alcibiades exhibits towards his now middle-aged teacher Socrates, who is also present. It seems that, after Pericles' death, Socrates had at first become a substitute father to Alcibiades, a mentor who could guide him in adult life. However, unlike the memory of Pericles that Alcibiades was delighted to try and honour in military glory, Socrates represented a very different role model – the model of someone who, through examining his actions, his thoughts and his character, sought not victories in war but wisdom of mind.

According to Plato, Alcibiades reacted violently against this. In the *Symposium* he testifies that, though he was moved by many of the great speeches of Pericles, none upset him so deeply as the things that Socrates said to him. In fact, Socrates shamed him:

> My very own soul started protesting that my life – my life! – was no better than the most miserable slave's. And yet that is exactly how this Marsyas here at my side makes me feel all the time: he makes it seem that my life isn't worth living! He always traps me, you see, and he makes me admit that my political career is a waste of time, while all that matters is just what I most neglect: my personal shortcomings, which cry out for the closest attention.

The tragedy for Alcibiades is that it is precisely this examination that he needs to undertake. He fails to do so. Plato continues with his psychological portrait of that failure by having Alcibiades vocalise his jealousy of Socrates' other students. Alcibiades is conflicted: he calls Socrates 'impudent, contemptuous and vile'. He is racked with a psychic pain that he describes as a 'snakebite of the soul'. The problem is that he is not able to question himself, as Socrates tried to encourage him to do.

Worse still, in another twist of his feelings for Socrates, Alcibiades tries to seduce him. And it is this obsession with his sexual and military prowess that reveals where Alcibiades went wrong in his relationships with these paternal figures. He refused to grow up. He refused to take responsibility for his own life. Instead, he was caught between trying to please two very different father-figures. It was never going to be possible. And it did not work.

What not to say

Plato saw where the roots of Alcibiades' downfall lay. As a result of not being reconciled to his family, he was condemned to repeat himself, with all the energy and charisma of a maniac, several times over in his life. He could talk about his agonies, but only as a capricious child. What he could not do was talk about them wisely, as an adult. He could only blame those around him, notably Socrates. He could not turn his powers of judgement upon himself and take responsibility for himself.

The lesson is as easy to state as it is hard to learn. When coping with families, what Alcibiades could not do is what we must strive for.

Having children

'Happy is the man that hath his quiver full of them.'   Psalms

What might be said

Here's an observation. There is something paradoxical about
people who have children. Rarely, it seems, do they ask why.
They ask how, at what cost, of what sex, with what names.
And of course, children become their own justification *after*
their extraordinary appearance, but that is to beg the question of 'why?'. It would seem to be a fascinating as well as
challenging one to pursue properly. For it is not obvious, as
those who defer lumpenly to genes assume.

The paradox is underlined because the people who do ask
the question seriously are typically those who cannot have
children, or have discovered that having children is not
straightforward.

A second observation. Children can divide friends.
Usually this happens accidentally: parents with new children
simply do not have as much time for old friends, and their
interests inevitably shift with such life-changing events.
Only sometimes do children actively drive a wedge between

41

friends, as when one couple has them and another cannot, or when people simply own up to not liking children much. Incidentally, this latter confession can be made by a parent too, when it seems doubly shocking, doubly divisive.

I think that these two observations go together because I suspect that children would be less of a problem if it were easier to talk about why people want to have them. If they become a stumbling block between friends, and in relationships, habitually avoiding the question of 'why?' does not help.

There are two reasons why the business of having children fascinates me, and why I am conscious that it is difficult to ask why. First, I have noticed that many couples have difficulty conceiving, or do not have children at all. The frequency is far higher than might at first be thought. At times, these individuals can feel burdened with a kind of a shame because of their childlessness. The word says it all: 'childless'. It sounds like an ancient curse – as if they had been denied a blessing from God. Similarly, it seems offensive to ask a couple why they do not have or want children, it feels like asking why they are selfish.

The second reason for wanting to talk about it is that I do not have children myself. Neither, hand on heart, could I say I would want them. The reasons for that are various and not always clear to me, but the point to highlight here is that even making such a confession feels as if I risk causing offence. I do not mean to, and I'd like to know why.

What is at stake

Bertrand Russell recognised the centrality of the question. In his guide to the good life, *The Conquest of Happiness,* parents and children have a chapter of their own. Entitled 'The Family', it comes in the part of his book that deals with the causes of happiness, as opposed to the causes of unhappiness that he dealt with earlier.

Russell notes that, in practice, nine times out of ten the relationship between parents and children is a source of disquiet. He knew all about it. He had tried to be a model father, and in his time was an important advocate of some of the latest theories of parenting – a veritable Gina Ford. But he married three times and his eldest son was so unhappy that he developed chronic mental illness.

The unhappiness to which families can give rise runs as deeply as the structures of society, Russell believed. It depends on factors as diverse, and tricky, as the emancipation of women and the planning of towns and cities. There is little that most individuals can do about such things; they are our lot, for good or ill. So why, does he think, most people persist in having children?

There are traditional reasons that might once have held sway, but that Russell thinks no longer obtain. For example, who today has children because they regard it as their civic duty? Or who has them because they believe that children are the reason that marriage was given by God?

However, there is a biological root to wanting children that is about as fundamental as you can get. Russell calls it the feeling of having 'one's own body externalised' – a physical, even carnal turn of phrase that captures something of the appeal of fecundity, and conversely, the fear of infertility. I recall one of my friends, for whom conceiving was not straightforward, saying that she realised she wanted children when she became conscious of the desire to extend the love that she found with her husband. It is a similar sentiment, having to do with wanting that love to grow and live on.

Russell also notes that it is only in the modern period that people have thought to question the happiness that children offer: 'Parenthood is psychologically capable of providing the greatest and most enduring happiness that life has to offer. This, no doubt, is more true of women than men, but is more true of men than most moderns are inclined to suppose.'

The wisdom of the ages would suggest that 'when circumstances lead men or women to forgo this happiness, a very deep need remains ungratified, and . . . this produces a dissatisfaction and listlessness of which the cause may remain quite unknown'. The reason for this, he suggests, is that there is a tremendous satisfaction to be found in contributing to the 'stream of life', to the culture and community that is the wellspring of our identity. This can be satisfied by worldly achievements, though inevitably few people are remembered in this way, for few are that distinguished. Therefore, a far better way of fulfilling this need for connection is in children. They are more than likely to remember you. And since to want to participate in the stream of life is basic and natural, it is arguably best realised in the basic and natural activity that having children is.

Children bring practical benefits that are hard to secure in other ways too. For example, Russell argues that they have the greatest chance of turning the parental generation's thoughts to the future, since the future belongs to the parental generation's children. This is of value in offsetting the selfish short-termism that might otherwise seek to satisfy only immediate desires. Having said that, there are sociologists who worry that the youth of the twenty-first century are themselves already a 'now-generation', training themselves not to delay gratification but take it at once – in, for example, the computer games they play.

What not to say

Russell's answers to the question are all debatable, of course. He commends the value of the parent–child connection because, although any other relationship might fail or let you down in a crisis, this one will persist. But is this insurance against isolation, or rather a recipe for disappointment?

Alternatively, it seems reasonable to debate whether children can satisfy the 'immortal longings' of their parents, be that in the extension of their love or in the desire to be remembered. Perhaps it is sensing this burden that so often causes children to rebel?

And it is worth asking whether Russell's children provided him with the happiness he sought from them. Given his family history, that seems questionable. That he included a chapter on the family in *The Conquest of Happiness* might say more about the triumph of hope over experience, than the ability of parenthood to provide the 'greatest and most enduring happiness that life has to offer'. And note the gruelling tone implicit in the word 'conquest'. Can happiness be happy when conquered?

But look! We have started a discussion. The question has been asked. Russell sets an agenda; he provides us with something to say. Ask it again. What do you think?

Coming out

'In everyone there sleeps / A sense of life lived according to love.'

Philip Larkin

What might be said

Perhaps coming out will always be a milestone, a rite of passage. Of course, you can hide your homosexuality, a deception that is simply not an option if you are left-handed or have red hair. And it is an exceptionally brave or foolish child who chooses not to conceal their minority status, if they can, during the playground years. One day they may sit down with Mum and/or Dad and initiate the conversation that begins: 'I've got something to tell you.' What are they going to say?

Even the ancient Greeks, for whom a same-sex affair was something all men ought to have at least once, thought it tricky. Young men were the epitome of beauty, but the moral conundrums their delightful appearance provoked were as much agonised about as celebrated. A bit like today's student who should get drunk but not be a drunk, lovers had to achieve the correct balance or they were liable to be the butt of jokes.

Periander's boy fumed when asked whether he was pregnant yet, and Socrates chastised another for rubbing himself like a pig against a stone, at least according to Xenophon.

Little wonder that even in a country like Britain that has recently achieved historic highs of tolerance, every lesbian or gay man will know of at least a few in their circle who are out with them but are not out at work, or to their family, or with other friends.

My coming-out story was relatively uneventful. I was in my late teens and I told my father first. I recall that his response was characterised by humility more than anything else. I don't think he liked the thought, and fought it for a while, but he also wanted to learn about what gayness meant. In time, he understood enough to find the grounds to embrace it.

My mother, who had guessed something was up, was upset. Not from revulsion but because she thought her son might be unhappy in love. And at one level, for some time, she was not wrong about that! I think that during my years in the closet I developed a habit of keeping my emotions to myself, for fear that they would give me away and provoke a violent response. So whilst politically my homosexuality was fully expressed, by being chair of the Gay Soc at university, for example, personally I remained reticent about any relationship until I was well into my mid-thirties.

Also, I have to confess that I rather liked the thought of myself as different, and having at least one feature that meant I might not be one of the herd. I increasingly realised, however, that that difference could at times be met with indifference – as it was when I told my siblings. I was the one who was then outraged; surely you could show some shock or surprise, I complained to myself.

What is at stake

The sexuality of the French philosopher, Michel Foucault, was for a long time something of a conundrum. For one of his biographers, David Macey, his homosexuality did nothing less than underpin his commitment to his own and others' freedom: it fuelled a visceral hatred of oppression, formed his *oeuvre* into a 'toolbox' against tyranny that contributed not only to gay liberation but also to penal reform and revisions of psychiatric treatments.

For another biographer, James Miller, Foucault's sexuality was not so much a source of inspiration as the key to unlocking the dark secrets of his esoteric thought. Miller wrote that Foucault was a tormented homosexual who attempted suicide, hated French society and sought extreme experiences – not least drugs and sadomasochistic sex, from which he probably contracted AIDS, the disease that killed him in 1984.

Didier Eribon, who was a friend, treats Foucault's homosexuality as a personal detail. He argues that it was difficult to bear in the 1940s when he came of age, and certainly coloured his relationship with his parents. But it should not detract from his status as France's leading thinker after Sartre. It was simply there. Eribon quotes Foucault as saying, 'Whenever I have tried to carry out a piece of theoretical work it has been on the basis of my own experience, always in relation to processes I saw taking place around me. It is because I thought I could recognise in the things I saw, in the institutions in which I dealt, in my relations with others, cracks, silent shocks, malfunctionings . . . that I undertook a particular piece of work, a few fragments of autobiography.'

A powerful motivation? A private perversion? A personal detail? What was Foucault's sexuality to him? The reason his biographers portray it so differently is that Foucault was pretty evasive about his homosexuality himself. In fact, he refused to come out, in the sense of making a public declaration of his gayness. Some thought this bizarre, as it was widely known that he had a male partner of over twenty years' standing. Others thought it hypocritical – typical of those who live in the ivory tower of academe and their hypocrisy when it comes to dealing with 'real life'.

However, Foucault had good reason to be hesitant about labelling himself gay. It had little to do with either fear or furtiveness. He believed that the modern obsession with sexuality, and the contemporary mania for expressing whether you are this or that, was itself a form of oppression. He called it the 'austere monarchy of sex', a regime that is arguably far more restrictive than that cultivated by the supposedly repressive Victorians.

This came into sharp focus for him one day at a seminar he gave in California. The seminar had gone well, and many students lingered afterwards, chatting and exploring the ideas that had been raised. Finally, just one attractive young man was left, yet finding himself alone with the professor he became agitated. Foucault asked him what was wrong, and the chap blurted out that he thought Foucault might make a pass at him and that he wouldn't know what to do. How sad, thought Foucault. Here was a lovely encounter – the very stuff of which the happy, intellectual life is made. And yet they couldn't enjoy it. It was ruined by the spectre of sex. Such is the oppression that, paradoxically, exists in a culture where your sexuality, and its 'liberation', is a defining characteristic of your life.

Everyone – gay, straight or somewhere in between – suffers because of such classifications. It is just that being gay makes you more aware of the ways in which they stop you being yourself, cajoling you to don certain stereotypes instead. Of course, sometimes it is fun to 'be gay' and throw tantrums or wear tiaras like Elton John, and gay pubs are an invaluable safe space long before they risk becoming a gay ghetto. But these things have to be kept in their place. Mark Simpson, a perceptive and droll writer on matters queer, points out that lesbians and gays can get trapped in their 'liberation'. It can become a kind of command to keep coming out – by, say, going on all the right parades, reading all the right novels, or being seen at the right clubs. Like the evangelical Christian who goes on and on about being saved, it is not only tedious but suggests a mono-dimensional, restrictive way of life.

What not to say

Foucault thought that the key to sexuality was not so much to come out as to find a way out of sexuality's constraints; less of the 'I am what I am', more of the 'I am not just gay'. This is tough, for ultimately it requires society to change too. But he thought that if you set a task of questioning yourself, imagining how things might be different and refusing to live by a label, you might make some progress.

In fact, gay people can turn their difference to their advantage. By virtue of having long noticed that they don't quite fit in, they are well placed to be at the vanguard of ways of life in which sexuality becomes a minor issue. 'We must escape and help others escape the two ready-made formulas of the pure sexual encounter and the lovers' fusion of identities,' Foucault said. Perhaps gay people can contribute to the invention of a new A-Z of friendship, he mused. He tried to do his bit with a philosophy that he described as an attempt to 'think differently'.

After all, people do not come out as an exercise in prurience, as if all they want is to confess that they like this or that. No. To come out is at last to say, 'I have sensed a life that is lived according to love.'

So if someone comes out to you, neither curse irately nor shrug your shoulders indifferently. Say, 'Do you know, I don't think I am quite what I seem either.'

Domestic violence

'A woman, let her be as good as she may, has got to put up with the life her husband makes for her.'   George Eliot

What might be said

Domestic violence and marital rape is a shockingly substantial, grossly ugly problem. The British Crime Survey records well over half a million incidents of domestic violence a year in the UK. Around 150 women are killed as a result. One in four women – and one in six men – are victims and it constitutes about a quarter of all violent crime. It is doubly dangerous because, unlike a theft or assault on the street, it is rarely a one-off incident. It is usually part of a pattern of on-going abusive behaviour.

So what do its victims, and those who suspect its presence, most commonly say? In a word, nothing. Domestic violence is massively under-reported. It is surrounded with stigma. The abused fear that they will not be believed or will make themselves more vulnerable. Friends and relatives commonly put indications of domestic violence down to other causes, or ignore them. They may well have never asked the person concerned. Abusers hide behind cultural, religious, financial and emotional barriers.

I was alerted to the cultural conspiracy that conceals domestic violence via a rather specialist concern, namely that of radical feminist theology. A professor at Boston College advised me to take the plunge and read the author Mary Daly. She was a colleague of his, though he had never heard her speak as she refused to admit men to her lectures.

Daly is an awkwardly witty, deadly serious writer. She focuses on the damage that religions do to women, particularly Christianity. Her argument is punchy and powerful: if God is male, as God the Father most certainly is, then the male is God. 'The character of Vito Corleone in *The Godfather* is a vivid illustration of the marriage of tenderness and violence so intricately blended in the patriarchal ideal,' she writes in *Beyond God the Father*.

Other theologians have contested Daly's claims, not least other feminist theologians. Some have pointed out that alongside the male images of God as Father and Son are the more ambiguous ones of God as Spirit. In the Old Testament, the Spirit of God is envisaged as a wise woman, Sophia – i.e. as a female figure.

But the challenge to Daly that interested me was more imaginative still. It stressed that at the heart of the Christian story is the image of God the Son dead on a cross, himself a victim of violence. Moreover, just before he dies, the Son cries out, 'My God, my God, why have you forsaken me?' In other words, like the abandoned victims of domestic violence, he is abandoned by a man, as it were, to the violence of men. The story transgresses the gender roles common in domestic violence.

This, it was argued, by other feminist theologians, is terrible and hopeful. To the believer, Jesus takes the place of suffering women – and makes redemption possible by beginning to break the cycle of violence. Mary Daly would argue that this idea is even more objectionable, suggesting that women must rely on men for their redemption. But she misses the point. In a twist of the plot that outdoes the barbarity of Mario Puzo's *Godfather*, this God-Father is complicit in the death of his Son. It is as if the perverse patriarchal ideal of 'tender violence' collapses under the weight of its own hideous contradiction. It places responsibility for the violence squarely on the shoulders of men.

What is at stake

Many people, far more qualified than I, have written about the silence that so often surrounds domestic violence. So, here, let us consider what feminist philosophy has to say about it.

The main problem feminist philosophers highlight is the social distinction between the public and the private spheres of existence. This is such a tricky issue because the division between public and private is central to many of the great goods of liberal politics. That there is a private realm into which politics should not stray preserves the individual's liberty; the rule of law regulates the public sphere, unless you live under a tyranny. The division is also reflected in the existence of 'no-go areas' for politicians. They are usually wary of laws that tell parents how to raise their children – witness the rows over smacking. They hesitate before legislating on what people should eat, the exercise they should take, and so on – for all that these things have an enormous impact upon, say, health budgets and a citizen's general well-being. Politicians who do launch into these areas leave themselves hostages to fortune; they are despised for their nanny-statism, and with good reason.

However, though the existence of a part of life over which the state has no legitimacy is vital for our freedom, feminists have shown how women are associated more strongly with this private sphere, notably in relation to the home. Being situated in this place means that sometimes they are beyond the help of the state, though by all other standards the law should intervene. The debate about whether mothers should receive remuneration for 'not working' and raising children is one aspect of this. For many men, the notion that they would engage in such intensive labour, let alone without financial reward, is simply unthinkable because, unlike women's, men's work somehow 'belongs' to the public sphere.

Similarly, domestic violence and marital rape have traditionally been considered personal matters. The law has hesitated in recognising these realities of women's lives because they are considered private. At an individual level too, many people's natural response, should they hear about domestic violence or suspect it is taking place, is to feel that they will not, perhaps should not, get involved. Thus it is in Noël Coward's play, notably entitled *Private Lives*, that Elyot can confess without fear of retribution, even as a kind of joke, 'Certain women should be struck regularly, like gongs.'

The British MP Harriet Harman, who has long campaigned against domestic violence, has stressed the importance of making it clear to men that assaulting a wife or girlfriend is a criminal act, i.e., one that does belong to the public sphere. 'There are many men who, though they assault their wives, do not consider themselves criminal – they are not like that,' she has said. 'They have good jobs and command respect. But if you commit assault at home you are every bit as much a criminal as someone who assaults a stranger in the street.'

So when people feel that such things must somehow be sorted out between the couple concerned, they overlook the fact that the woman's lack of power, because the situation is regarded as private, lies at the root of the problem. Someone – state or friend – must intervene, must breach the divide between the public and private. Only then can the woman be helped, justice be done and lives saved. The personal is political.

What not to say

For this reason, much of the effort in tackling domestic violence is spent on encouraging people to speak out. Support is offered. Protection is afforded. Advice is given. So seek out that support, protection and advice. For in the striking three words of feminists and campaigners, it is still too often the case that 'silence is death'.

Handling depression

'The trick is to keep breathing.'   Janice Galloway

What might be said

It seems that nothing works when someone is depressed. If they are merely sad you can be jolly, and some of your jests will make them smile. If they are distressed you can comfort them, and your concern will ease their disquiet.

But when someone is depressed, merriment will only deepen their sense of melancholia. Love cannot mitigate it; in fact, anything you might say can be taken in the wrong way or thoughtlessly rejected.

This is why it is easy to become angry with someone who is depressed, as heartless as that may seem to the outsider.

Speaking personally, I have been depressed – 'properly' depressed, as opposed to sad or distressed – just once in my life. What was peculiar about this period was that for a long time I did not know I was depressed. Certainly, I felt low and without energy. I recall feeling as if I was being pushed, face first, hard against a wall. The force behind me was such that not only could I not take a step back, I couldn't even lower myself to see whether there was a way underneath it.

However, it was not until I told a friend that I was in the habit of going to bed at lunchtime and sleeping until five or six – and they were brave enough to say, 'You are depressed' – that I realised something substantial was wrong. They wisely did not say much more. Instead, they had the grace to listen to my pitiful confession of astonishment that this condition could have crept up on me.

That they sat with me was, in retrospect, the beginning of the end of my depression. I gained just enough of an insight into the way I was living to take steps to re-orientate it. I also see now that I had not gone over the edge, as psychotic depressives do, though I had seen enough of that black hole from afar to have real sympathy for those who disappear into it.

Interestingly, I think that this depression was different from another occasion, a few years later, when I had a minor breakdown. The presenting symptoms then were that for about a week I could do nothing without crying. I could not answer the phone without choking. Or, when I briefly left the house to buy a carton of milk, I had to do so without speaking, in case I began to weep.

However, I do not think I was depressed during this period. I knew I was profoundly unhappy, to the extent that I was incapable of functioning, but although it took me a while to recover I knew that I would do so, given time. In other words, the breakdown had meaning, in that it was cathartic. Depression is so deadly because it has no meaning at all.

What is at stake

Depression does not always have psychological causes. It can, as Sigmund Freud put it, have 'somatic' origins: it might be a matter of chemistry and neurons not childhood and neurosis. The way to tackle somatic depression is with drugs and other physiological procedures. However, even in these cases, the sufferer will still *feel* depressed; the 'black dog', as Samuel Johnson first named his bouts of despair, is nothing if not an experience. So Freud's attempt to map depression subjectively is valuable in attempting to appreciate what is at stake in all cases.

To open up the experience of depression, Freud draws an analogy with profound mourning. The loss of someone who was keenly loved is a useful way into understanding depression because it is an experience many will have had or can imagine. It has a number of typical characteristics. These include a painful frame of mind, a loss of interest in the outside world, an inability to care much for anyone else. Freud uses the word 'pain' a number of times in his description, a strikingly physical feeling for an essentially interior experience. But that is what mourning is like. He also notes that profound mourning can become so exclusive a devotion to the one lost, and to the mourning itself, that it 'leaves nothing over for other purposes or other interests'. For example, when Constance loses her son, in Shakespeare's play *King John*, she is accused of loving mourning as much as she loved him. The accusation is right: mourning has become her way of loving her son. She replies: 'Grief fills the room up of my absent child, Lies in his bed, walks up and down with me.'

Such is the darkly all-consuming, plunging nature of mourning. Depression – or melancholia, as Freud calls it – is very much like it, except for one key difference. Mourning can find a resolution when, instead of trying to maintain a hopeless connection with the lost loved one, the mourner comes to terms with the loss and finds a new way of loving them – notably in memories. It may be a horrid struggle. But it is something that most achieve; mourners learn to be happy again *and* remain conscious of their loss.

Depression differs because the melancholic is entirely unclear about the causes of their sadness and how it might be resolved. Typically it appears to have nothing to do with the outside world; it has no trigger like the loss of a loved one. Depression turns in on itself; it is a solipsistic experience in which the individual doubts themselves. It is the moment of Hamlet's nihilistic contemplation: 'To be, or not to be: that is the question.'

This is puzzling to the concerned observer of the depressive. How can they doubt themselves? It makes no sense. Are they not loved? What this third party can miss, for all their care, is that the melancholic suffers from 'an extraordinary diminution in his self-regard, an impoverishment of his ego on a grand scale'. Freud continues: 'In mourning it is the world which has become poor and empty; in melancholia it is the ego itself. The patient represents his ego to us as worthless, incapable of any achievement and morally despicable; he reproaches himself, vilifies himself and expects to be cast out and punished.' The individual may not sleep or eat, and most dramatically of all, may lose the instinct to cling to life.

This is why the best that depressives may manage to

achieve is simply to cope with one moment at a time. 'The trick is to keep breathing,' was Janice Galloway's formula, and the title of her novel. Gerard Manley Hopkins caught the negativity differently when he wrote, in 'Carrion Comfort', of the meagre hope of a day when he might 'not choose not to be'.

Freud put melancholia down to a violent self-disregard. Depressives become embroiled in a brutal, self-obsessed pattern of judging and being judged. Any objective assessment of the injustice they mete out to themselves in their self-condemnation is irrelevant. The depressive does not know why; they only know what is, to them. And that reality is worthlessness. They cannot imagine what it might be to be happy, which someone who is mourning can at least conceive of doing some time in the future.

What not to say

Freud suggests several things that, though apparently obvious to the outsider, are useless when said to the seriously depressed. For example, it is fruitless to contradict them in their self-loathing. That is how they feel: they *are* lacking in interest, love and ambition. Indeed, it might be best to confirm them in that sensibility, since at least it establishes a connection across their otherwise total withdrawal from the world.

More profoundly, there is a kind of wisdom in melancholia. If someone condemns themselves as weak, narcissistic or dishonest, they are tapping into a partly true perception of the human condition. This is one reason why depression can be so frightening to the observer: 'We only wonder that a man has to be ill before he can be accessible to a truth of this kind,' Freud muses. In other words, even if everyone else would judge them as good, that is a meaningless endorsement to the depressive.

Another troubling aspect of depression is that sufferers are immune to the comfort that their self-criticism is unjustified. So there is little point in offering it. Conversely, to demand that they pull themselves together is the worst thing to say since it will be heard as another strike of the judge's hammer upon the sentencing block.

The one thing that someone can do with a depressive is be alongside them. It is essential to explore medical interventions, since the depression might be somatic, at least in part. Drugs may also help to break the cycles of self-loathing. And there are other techniques, like Cognitive Behavioural Therapy, that may assist someone in managing their depression – if they can summon up the energy to act against their own despair. But for deep psychological depression, the only possible way out is the slow, time-consuming healing of the talking cure. The factors that are unconscious might be glimpsed; and thus objectified, the patient may be loosened from their grip.

Facing suicide

'Guns aren't lawful; nooses give; gas smells awful; you might as well live.'   Dorothy Parker

What might be said

The thought of suicide may come in several guises. There is the suicidal desire of the person who is profoundly depressed. There is the suicidal cry of the person who actually seeks help to live. There is the wish of the person with an incurable disease for a doctor to assist them in an early death. All pose a tremendous challenge to a person searching for the right thing to say.

However, arguably the most alarming situation of all is the cool and calculated suicide of a rational individual. They will conclude their business. They will compose a note – before cutting short their life.

This situation differs from the depressed suicide, where those who are left at least know there was a reason for their loved one's death. As it does from the cry for help, since there is the hope that this suicide attempt will be half-hearted and the help sought subsequently found. And with euthanasia, there is at least a moral problem to grapple with, coupled to the hope that death lies a little within human control.

A rational suicide, though, forces us to stare into the abyss. A terrible 'why?' echoes across the lives of those who live on. Such a death never kills just one person. It mortally wounds those around them too.

When the Samaritans, and other telephone helplines, sift new applications for volunteers, there is one role-play that sorts the wheat from the chaff. It is role-playing the suicide call. Actually, very few of those who make calls to the Samaritans do so because they are contemplating suicide. For a couple of years I was a volunteer on a similar service, called Nightline, and never once spoke to anyone in such desperate straits. However, it is always a possibility, and this is a good role-play because of the extremity of the situation. With all calls, there is the risk that the volunteer might be a hindrance rather than a help. If the caller is a would-be suicide and the conversation goes wrong, that damage can never be undone.

During the role-play, the listener faces two questions. First, what would they do if they suspected someone was committing suicide whilst they were on the phone? Would they inform the police, trace the call and send an ambulance? Or would they respect the wishes of the suicidal person and leave them to die?

There is no wrong or right answer, but what that question leads to is the second one, which is less theoretical and much closer to home. How would they feel if someone died whilst they were talking to them? Contemplating that possibility is what often helps an applicant decide whether they really want to volunteer.

What is at stake

'There is really only one serious philosophical problem, namely suicide.' This is the icy proposition with which Albert Camus begins his book, *The Myth of Sisyphus*. Sisyphus was a crafty character of Greek legend. When he was about to die, he told his wife not to offer the usual sacrifices. She obeyed, and now in the underworld before its queen, Persephone, Sisyphus complained that his wife was deserting her duty and that he should be allowed to return to Corinth to rectify the situation. Persephone obliged and, home again, Sisyphus refused to return. However, he did not escape. He was dragged back by Hermes, and condemned to manhandle a rock to the top of a hill, only to have it slip from his grasp just before the summit, forcing him to begin again, for all eternity.

The myth came to symbolise the labours of human life and their perpetual frustration, and it has been constantly reinterpreted to express various vanities. Lucretius applied it to the life of the politician, which is driven by the empty desire to exercise power and always ends in defeat.

Camus's essay on Sisyphus is the most memorable of the modern interpretations. This time the vanity is the search for meaning in a world that has killed God. Camus recognises that this act has thrown us into a crisis that revolves around the absurdness of life. It seems to us like hauling the rock must have seemed to Sisyphus: absolutely no way to live. Hence the rational option of suicide.

Camus does not, however, actually advocate suicide. Rather, he finds reason to keep on with the struggle, for the very reason that it is absurd. Human beings may have to acknowledge the limits of their understanding of the meaning of life, but they can also revolt against the emptiness with which such limitations constantly threaten us. 'What counts is not the best living but the most living,' he writes. Sisyphus is such a hero because, in spite of the utter futility of his existence, he still hates death and insists on living. His choice is full of dignity – the dignity of those who deny fate its capacity to destroy them. In fact, Sisyphus wins a kind of certainty: the absurdity of his plight. Thus, as he turns around to descend from the mountain again, Camus insists that we must think of Sisyphus as happy.

Camus's essay is a response to a particularly extreme type of existential crisis. By contemplating suicide, he actually conjures up a reason to live. He is like Marc Antony in Shakespeare's *Antony and Cleopatra*, who explains that, 'Fortune knows we scorn her most when most she offers blows.' Suicide remains a possibility, but now as a comfort, echoing Nietzsche's thought: 'With it a calm passage is to be made across many a bad night.' It helps people reach another day.

What not to say

Suicide has been dismissed as merely bringing forward the inevitable. This might be a humane way of regarding euthanasia, but in the cases when death is not naturally imminent, a 'successful' suicide is infinitely worse than such a glib phrase allows. It puts death before life. It destroys others. It cannot even laugh at the absurdity of life as a minimal reason to live. Perhaps this was why religious authorities used to condemn it.

You may disagree, but I would say that everything should be done to resist another's suicidal wishes. There will probably be nothing you can do with the required haste about the depression causing suicidal urges, but there may be much you can do to actually stop them dying. I would call the police and not listen to someone taking the pills or applying the knife. I would advise that if you think someone might be contemplating killing themselves, you should raise the subject and counter it. You will do no harm – they will have already thought extensively about the end themselves – and you may, in the long term, do much good.

Terminal news

'Illness is not something a person has; it's another way of being.'

Jonathan Miller

What might be said

During medieval times, it was the plague that filled people's hearts with fear. Then, in the early modern period, conditions like tuberculosis became coupled to the spectre of death. Today, cancer is the diagnosis that no one wants to hear, along with the grim terms of its associated vocabulary: 'malignant', 'metastasise', 'spread', 'terminal'. They powerfully impute life's frailty.

It is hard to know what to say to people who have received such news because there is apparently no hope to draw on. We fall back on a few stock sentiments. People with cancer are urged to fight it, to enjoy what time remains, to learn to live with it. Terminal illness may bring out the best in people. Or the worst.

However, the thing that has struck me in seeing several people I have loved cope with terminal illness is the way that it inverts life. Those who do not know what will kill them live life forwards, towards an indefinite number of tomorrows. Those who do know what will kill them live life backwards, from the day that they will die. They see life from the other end. And it is this, I suspect, that lies at the root of another experience people have upon receiving such ghastly news; paradoxically, they feel extraordinarily alive. As Dennis Potter put it, whilst he sipped morphine, he no longer just saw the blossom on the apple tree outside his window: 'I see the whitest, frothiest, blossomest blossom that there ever could be. The nowness of everything is absolutely wondrous. If you see the present tense – boy, do you see it. And boy, do you celebrate it.'

Why does the prospect of death do this?

There are a handful of scientists today who say that the baby has already been born who will live for 1,000 years. Whatever the truth of that, the first generation of the twenty-first century can reasonably expect to enjoy 100 birthdays, possibly 200. However, the real goal of the science of longevity is not the extension of life but the elixir of life – the technology that might make us live for ever.

It is an ancient aspiration. Stealing the gift of everlasting life from the gods is a regular motif in ancient myth. Christianity developed a different nuance: people would die, but if they were saved they would rise again with incorruptible bodies. Science, therefore, is just continuing the tradition, if with more material means.

The hope of immortality has been revived because research suggests that the human body actually stops ageing, if at the somewhat belated age of about ninety. As Bryan Appleyard points out in *How to Live Forever or Die Trying*, we do not die but are killed. So, if the things that kill us could be eliminated – with medicine, nanotechnology and physiologically optimised lifestyles – then we need not die. If people could remain perpetually at around the age of thirty – physically vigorous, mentally mature – then the dream of the ages would be achieved.

Now, it could be that such science is deluded or wildly optimistic. Like accelerating a mass to the speed of light, immortality might require powers of medicine that are effectively infinite. However, imagine for a minute that you could have it. Would you want to live for ever?

What is at stake

Seneca, the Roman stoic philosopher, wrote an essay entitled 'On the Shortness of Life'. He lived at a time when death lurked at every turn, because of disease and political disquiet. He knew the Grim Reaper in two guises. First, in that he suffered from ill-health and lost his first wife in childbirth; the happiness of pregnancy was clouded by the fear of death for women throughout most of human history. Second, in that what killed Seneca were the tempestuous whims of his master, the emperor Nero, at whose command he committed suicide in 65 CE.

His essay begins practically. 'It is not that we have a short time to live, but that we waste a lot of it. Life is long enough, and a sufficiently generous amount has been given to us for the highest achievements if it were all well invested.' In other words, the problem is not that life is short. It is that we make it short. We waste it, as thoroughly as gamblers waste their wealth.

The reason we do this, according to Seneca, is that we live as if we were destined to live for ever. Like a teenager who cannot be bothered to leave his bed all morning, presuming that there are endless mornings to come, we squander life as if we had an endless supply of it. People say they will retire at sixty and *then* live the life they would choose. 'How late it is to begin really to live just when life must end,' Seneca cries. Apart from the fact that sixty years of life will have formed and probably fixed your character, leaving you with few choices as to how subsequently to live, there is no guarantee that you will make retirement, even with medical advances.

In fact, medical advances might come at a cost in terms of living to the full. A life that is apparently without threat conceals its swiftness as it glides quietly by. The result: 'You have been preoccupied whilst life hastens on. Meanwhile, death will arrive, and you have no choice in making yourself available for that.'

Seneca's advice is to try to live within the sphere over which you have control, that is now. The past is gone; the future is uncertain; only now can be lived. It is perhaps this sense of 'now', the result of the shock of seeing life from the other end, that is the thorny gift of a terminal illness.

A strong sense of nowness deepens life for a number of reasons. Consider happiness. Happiness depends upon memories, not for reasons of nostalgia but because to be happy, at least in part, is to see that your life has goals, shape and purpose – memories being the means to take stock of it. It is for this reason that the Greeks used to say that someone couldn't be happy until they were on their death-bed; only then could they see their life complete and so enjoy its felicity. In other words, though we must live our lives forwards, happiness is gained by assessing it backwards. The implication is that without any consciousness of the end from which to look back, happiness will elude us.

Or what about the part that nowness might play in love? The idea here is not so much that the love shared with an eternal partner would inevitably dull over time. More, it is that to love someone is to long to be with them. This carries the corollary that love deepens with the possibility that you will not be together some day; parting makes the heart grow fonder, as they say. So death is a kind of guarantee of love, and people who are dying often inspire the greatest love.

What not to say

So who wants to live for ever? The person who has received news of a terminal illness may well wish they could, at least at first. But perhaps, as the reality of their situation sinks in, the nowness of the good life might emerge. Coupled to inevitable sadness, about the things they will miss or can no longer do, their disease could enable them to live in a way they have never managed before.

What, then, to say? The person with a terminal illness might be glad of your efforts to cheer them up, or encourage their fight, on occasion. But do not let that kind of talk distance you from another possibility: in reminding you of your own death, their situation might be a gift to you too. Their nowness might become yours. Their way of seeing the blossom could enliven your seeing.

As for the contemporary dreams of immortality through the power of science, I, for one, am cautious. Cures as a goal are obviously a good thing, but nurturing the hope that death itself might be avoidable could have dangerous side-effects. It might inure you against living. Happiness, love and the ability to live 'presently' might slip from your grasp. To borrow Seneca's phrase again: lengthening life might paradoxically shorten it.

Personal crisis

'Yet being – what is being? It "is" It itself.'   Martin Heidegger

What might be said

Profound depression is a causeless, shapeless despair that drenches life with its damp chill, as thoroughly as a fog rolling off the sea. It can no more be reasoned away than people can pull themselves off the ground by their shoe laces. But there are other crises in life that are amenable to reason. These crises fall into the category known as 'existential', being about who or what or how we are. They might be provoked by a soulless job, an empty marriage or a vacuous way of life. It is like realising that the compass needle you had been religiously following is not pointing north – but east, or is it west? That which had orientated you has become drained of meaning; it can no longer provide any bearings.

For a while, people who are having such a crisis may feel depressed, but generally speaking, if you talk with them, they can find something to say about it even during their worst lows. Although it will almost certainly not be the fundamental cause of their trouble, they can focus their crisis on their job, or marriage, or way of life – and so begin to find cause and shape. Like Jean-Paul Sartre, they are acquainted with ennui, but can also be persuaded that 'Human life begins on the far side of despair' – if only they can find a way to it. That is the challenge for the person who seeks to help; who must work out what to say.

When speaking with someone having an existential crisis there is a danger of latching too firmly on to the presenting symptoms – the job, marriage or way of life – and presuming that if these can be fixed, the crisis can be fixed too. That, though, is probably wrong. As the existentialist philosophers realised, the real problem is being itself. Unless this deeper crisis of life is confronted the symptoms will re-emerge, and the individual concerned will be condemned to repeat their behaviour time and time again.

The difficulty is that when being itself is the crisis, it resists resolution. How could it be otherwise should existence come to feel so determined, intransigent, irksome?

Existentialists say we are 'thrown' in to being, seized by it. There is no escape (or only one, suicide, which is not part of the kind of crisis we are examining here).

The insoluble nature of being itself is why it is tempting to focus only on the symptoms. In comparison, jobs, marriages and so on are child's play. They can in fact be changed. This is why, I suspect, much of the self-help movement and many of the life-coaching programmes that one can sign up to encourage precisely this form of action. They work on the surface, re-organising the symptoms in the hope that they might become less troubling and more manageable. Each has a different technique; each might really be an avoidance strategy. They fill your time, keep you occupied, don't let you stand still – which is why too, they can be so exhausting. You are not living, you are living the programme! But if the real challenge is existential, in time the self-help and the coaching will come to feel more oppressive than liberating, more like a sticking-plaster than a cure.

What is at stake

Our being – our existence – is a brute fact; it is possible to deny everything in life but that we are alive. Most of the time, though, we do not realise that we are alive in any deep sense. We are in the flow of life and it feels fine, more or less. An existential crisis is when the anxiety or absurdity of being hits us. It is like the bow of the boat in which we sit unexpectedly colliding with a hidden rock. If we'd been more alert we would have seen that it was there, its presence revealed by the slight undulations on the surface. The undulations are like the symptoms of the existential crisis. It is the immovable rock of being that is the fundamental problem.

The French philosopher and mathematician René Descartes can be thought of as the first person in the modern period to pay serious attention to the undulations and, instead of trying to avoid them, peer beneath the surface. He did it in his famous meditation in which he systematically doubted everything in his life, and arrived at the one thing he could not doubt, namely that he was doubting. Hence his famous maxim: 'I think therefore I am'. This was the bedrock of his existence, being itself.

However, other philosophers began to doubt the firm, if minimal, foundations upon which Descartes sought to rest. Later, Sartre argued that there is no such thing as thinking in isolation. Thinking must be directed at something else: it has content and so inevitably contemplates an object. Even pure thought is something that might be shared by someone else and so, in a sense, exists objectively, apart from the fact that we have had it. So, according to Sartre, Descartes's consciousness of himself in thought is, in fact, a delusion. Consciousness is only something if it is filled with things that come from the world. (It is this riddle that the *Matrix* films play on. We presume that our experience and our thoughts can unequivocally be called our own, whereas actually they could be generated by some matrix that contains us and is, therefore, more real than us.)

There is another way of reading Descartes that I think more successfully tackles the existential crisis. Descartes is usually taken as launching the philosophical project that searches for certainty in the human mind. Philosophers before him had looked for certainty in the world around them, perhaps in God or Platonic forms. Descartes, though, looked for what John Henry Newman called 'certitude', an internal state of consciousness that unquestionably stands fast. The fact that he did not find a form of certitude that has not subsequently been challenged suggests that he did not solve the existential crisis but deepened it.

However, this reading of Descartes ignores something else about his meditations. He took them to be proofs of God. What he meant, I think, is that it is clearly ridiculous to conclude that the only thing you can be sure of is that you are thinking. This is like the famous comment of Samuel

Johnson, when challenged to refute Bishop Berkeley's doctrine of the non-existence of matter, even the rocks and the stones. As James Boswell writes in his *Life*: 'I never shall forget the alacrity with which Johnson answered, striking his foot with mighty force against a large stone, till he rebounded from it – "I refute it thus."' Or as my grandmother, who was wise and pragmatic, once wrote: 'If there are many reasons to doubt things, there are many reasons not to doubt them too.'

In other words, Descartes's meditation is not so much a reflection on the uncertainties associated with the world in which we live, as a lesson on the limits of what we can say about the world in which we live. The world and our experience of being in it is ultimately a mystery. It is as strange as thinking about why there is something rather than nothing. And for Descartes this was a proof of God, since if we cannot comprehend these things there must surely be some being that can. That being must be beyond being to do so, and therefore divine.

This may strike you as sophistry in terms of proving the existence of God. Personally, I would say that was right. However, that failure does not detract from the success Descartes had in embracing the inherently limited capacity of the human mind to comprehend its own being. Clearly, human beings do understand much in certain areas of existence, like those that can be investigated by science. However, these tend to be the objective aspects of existence, not the subjective ones that cause an existential crisis. It is this ultimately insurmountable problem that Descartes grappled with in such an arresting way. What he achieves in his meditation – on the other side of his crisis – is not a proof of certainty but a sense of tranquillity amidst the doubt. His direction of travel is like the negative capability of John Keats: 'Negative Capability, that is when man is capable of being in uncertainties, mysteries, doubts, without any irritable reaching after fact and reason.'

What not to say

To be capable of being in uncertainty is, then, to have overcome an existential crisis. It may be that some things associated with the presenting symptoms will change too. In fact, it is very likely that they should, given that so much of life is 'lost in living', as T. S. Eliot put it. However, it is the plunge beneath the surface that needs to be embraced if life itself is to be recovered.

So what of the guide, the person who is alongside someone in such a crisis? What might they say? Clearly, there is no universal formula. Such a crisis is nothing if not personal. However, perhaps the figure of Socrates can help. He was another philosopher who sought to live with doubt. His wisdom was not that he knew much but that he understood how little he knew. 'I know one thing for sure,' he used to say, 'that really I know nothing.' This was his plunge. He sought to develop a way of life, subsequently called philosophy, that opened him up to the profound implications of such a crisis. That was why he irritated so many people in ancient Athens: in his life, he threatened their own reaching out after fact and reason, their own resistance to the question of being itself.

Yet someone who can conjure up a similar humility and

honesty has all they need to face the mystery. Another existentialist philosopher, Paul Tillich, called it simply and powerfully, 'the courage to be'.

Debating art

'Art is a jealous mistress.'   Ralph Waldo Emerson

What might be said

Have you ever wondered why most people are silent as they leave the cinema, art gallery or concert hall? Sometimes the silence is understandable: after a *Schindler's List* or Picasso's 'Guernica' it feels wholly appropriate. But mostly the silence is not out of respect or horror. At least in Britain, the atmosphere that accompanies the quiet exit is one of reserve or withholding. It is as if people daren't vocalise what they are thinking. Perhaps they do not know what to say beyond a banal platitude, and do not want to be exposed as so obvious a critic. Or maybe they fear that saying what they really thought would cause offence.

This suspicion seems proven on the occasions when someone, rebelling against the etiquette, does speak out. Their words fall into one of two categories. They are either bland: 'I thought her last one was better.' (Silence.) 'Well, I enjoyed that.' (Silence.) 'Why couldn't there have been a happy ending?' (Silence.) Or they appear designed deliberately to irritate: 'A five-year-old could have done better.' 'Well, of course, that was just a gloss on Baudrillard.' 'It just goes to prove what I have always said: nothing good has happened in music since 1974.' 1974?

Art is controversial. It always was. Plato banned poets in his ideal city because he thought they would cause division. There is a puritan religiosity – as old as the Bible – that is wary of art, believing that it battles with God for the rights to truth. Art sparks arguments about elitism. Tempers run high as one person relishes the genius and another laughs at the emperor's new clothes. In April 2007, there was a major retrospective opening in Tate Modern, London's 'Temple to Modern Art' – 'temple' meant disparagingly and exaltedly in equal measure. It features the artistic duo Gilbert and George. A typical move for them is to make faux religious images in stained glass that incorporate well-known four-letter words. To me it's childish; barely theologically literate. Or maybe I don't understand it. Because to others the work cuts through religious pretension with a devilishly sharp knife.

Certainly, in the modern world, art's shock value has become closely aligned with its intrinsic value. Is this why most people don't like to say anything as they leave the gallery or theatre? The unwritten rule is: 'don't meddle with it – just consume it', unless you can brave the maelstrom.

Yasmina Reza's play *Art* explores the relationship-destroying potential of art. The very simplicity of her title – the one word 'Art', i.e. nothing less than the whole business – underlines the idea that interpersonal disagreement is intrinsic to public aesthetics.

The plot concerns three friends. Serge buys a painting, at great expense. It is a white, featureless canvas. Marc can't believe it: 'You've paid two hundred thousand francs for this shit,' he spits. Yvan tries to moderate the row about the painting, for the sake of their friendship, but only succeeds in himself becoming an object of scorn – on Serge's part because Yvan won't support him, on Marc's part because he refuses to be honest about the work's vacuity.

Art leads to powerful feelings of betrayal. It is a catalyst that exposes the ugly side of each individual's character. The purchase yanks them out of complacency and calls their friendships into question: when confronted with something important, people cannot talk civilly about it, let alone decide. Their relationships unravel as a result.

The moral of the story is this: 'do' art at your peril.

What is at stake

The philosophy of art is a mass of subtle distinctions, ranging from the details of aesthetics to the question of what might count as art – and, of course, what does not. There is always scope for disagreement. However, there is one thing that seems indisputable: great art has a power; it moves you. Like George Bush or nuclear warfare, over which it is impossible not to have an opinion, it is its powerfulness that raises the stakes.

John Ruskin is one art critic who understood this and thought art was worth fighting over. Many critics would not agree with the details of Ruskin's aesthetics today. Indeed, he might be thought rather out of fashion, but his critical system demonstrates how deep art goes.

Modern Painters is his five-volume study of landscape painting and in it he articulates what he thought was at stake. The power of the book itself is indicated by the fact that, before Ruskin published it, art critics were inclined to think that the later paintings of Turner – with their huge swirls of ethereal colour – were crass. With *Modern Painters*, Ruskin turned that opinion around. Now Turner is regarded as one of Britain's greatest artists. (Incidentally, Ruskin did the same for Venice: before *The Stones of Venice* appeared, it was generally thought to be a rather ugly city; afterwards, a place of exquisite glory.)

The theme of *Modern Painters* can be summed up as the imperative in art of being true, in this case being true to nature. Nature was so important to Ruskin because he thought of it as the second great revelation of God, the first being the Bible. Art was therefore as crucial as theology; bad art as corrupting as heresy. 'To see clearly is poetry, prophecy and religion – all in one,' he wrote. The great painter of nature is one who reveals the truth of creation. This is what Turner's impressionism achieved. Inferior work is false and, moreover, of dubious ethical value.

Ruskin's moral view of art was controversial in his own time not so much because of his appeal to the divine, an appeal that he later doubted himself, but because he understood being truthful to nature in a radically different way from the matter of accurate representation, as we today see in a photograph. This raised the question of how the veracity of Turner's paintings could possibly be judged. Simultaneously, he accused his own critics of parroting convention because they viewed Turner solely by comparison with contemporaries, and thereby found him wanting.

They didn't understand him because he was new, Ruskin in effect declared – echoing the common defence of all modern art.

From high theology, to aesthetic judgement, to personal attack: this is the range of sensitivities that become targets when discussing art. It is unsurprising that people might choose to keep quiet.

What not to say

Art criticism has moved on since Ruskin. His version of modernity, captured in the true-to-nature slogan that was so novel at the time, now seems hopelessly conservative. Picasso developed the thought when he said that art is not truth, but a lie that reveals truth. Others have abandoned the connection with truth, preferring instead to think about art in terms of its relationship with beauty, iconoclasm or wealth.

None of these has defused the antagonism, however, and it is still risky to talk about great art. Even Andy Warhol couldn't break the link. He was an anti-Romantic, about as far from Ruskin and the belief that art can connect as can be imagined. He strove to produce work that was flat, dull and meaningless – and sparked a wave of controversy that was all his own.

What not to wear

'Fashion is what you adopt when you don't know who you are.'

Quentin Crisp

What can be said

It goes without saying that Trinny and Susannah have the first and last word on what not to wear. For the best advice on coping, as they put it, with 'big tits' or 'saddlebags' I defer to them. Where philosophy can help is perhaps with the related problem of what to say when people ask, 'How do I look?' Indeed, Trinny and Susannah have made a career out of doing what most people dare not: they answer honestly.

Why is it so hard to find a kind response to a size 12 bum in a size 10 skirt? Why is it that to say you dislike the novel someone is reading is merely to pass comment, whereas to say you dislike their shirt is to insult them? Unless you live in North Korea, where government agents enforce the wearing of hair in accordance with the 'socialist lifestyle', we need not fear the fashion police. They may not exist, but we do. As novelist Elizabeth Bowen put it: 'On the subject of dress almost no one, for one or another reason, feels truly indifferent: if their own clothes do not concern them, some-body else's do.' Why?

The answer is that, more than most people like to admit, you are what you wear. The personal is political. And, so are the pashmina, the pedal-pushers, the plus-fours and the pinafore.

What people are wearing has always elicited excellent retorts for the very reason that clothes say so much about an individual. When Elizabeth Hurley famously appeared at a film premiere wearing a dress composed of little more than twenty-four safety pins, Toby Young commented: 'No one noticed Elizabeth Hurley until she put her clothes on.' A former leader of the British Labour Party, Michael Foot, did not own an item of clothing costing more than £99, until he was ridiculed for wearing a duffle coat on Remembrance Day at the Cenotaph that made him look like Paddington bear. Within twenty-four hours he had bought a dress coat costing £500. Or, when Nicole Kidman divorced Tom Cruise, she wickedly commented: 'Now I can wear heels.'

What is at stake

Clothing features surprisingly frequently in the history of philosophy. The Victorian philosopher Robert Carlyle's first big book was called *Sartor Resartus* or 'The Tailor, Re-tailored'. It featured a complete philosophy of clothes, though should you read it for tips it would not be much help today. Clothes are a metaphor for shifting cultural phenomena. The philosophy is really about the way mean-ing, fashion and beliefs constantly change.

An anti-philosophy of clothes might be said to be part of the legacy of none other than Socrates. Ask an ancient Athenian what they knew about him, and they would probably not have said he was a philosopher. They would more likely have said that he wore no shoes, dressed shabbily and washed infrequently. On the day he was executed, one of his friends fetched him a fine robe, the more elegantly in which to expire. 'I have lived all my life in these clothes and now you tell me they are not good enough to die in,' he quipped.

The personal nature of our apparel, and the reason it is so hard to say the right thing when someone gets it wrong, is well expressed by one of the best dressed thinkers of the modern period, Oscar Wilde. His philosophy of the individual highlights the two issues that raise the stakes.

First, appearances count. 'It is only the shallow people who do not judge by appearances.' Wilde wrote this in *The Picture of Dorian Gray*, the story of a man who doesn't age because his portrait in the attic does. Many would disagree, arguing exactly the opposite, that you should *not* judge by appearances. 'If most of us are ashamed of shabby clothes and shoddy furniture, let us be more ashamed of shabby ideas and shoddy philosophies,' opined Albert Einstein, adding somewhat grimly: 'It would be a sad situation if the wrapper were better than the meat wrapped inside it.'

If you don't believe that appearances count imagine the Pope in a pair of Levis or the Queen in a shell-suit; such pictures in the paper would cause outrage. Or think of the storm that is unleashed when two celebrities appear at a gala wearing the same frock. The façade of their uniqueness seems to crumble, their semi-divine status is smashed; no longer are they the stunning creations that dazzle us. It is as if the manufactured nature of the whole business is exposed.

Some people will say that they don't care what they look like. If they look scruffy or dreary, then so be it. But that attitude is itself a statement – perhaps against fashion or against a culture fixated on presentation. What it underlines again is that appearances do count. As Mark Twain said, 'Clothes make the man. Naked people have little or no influence on society.'

Second, style is character. If appearances count, they do so for mixed reasons. It is, in part, because we live in a so-called post-modern world where depth and meaning seem to be heavily eroded, and culture is often little more than a shallow play on the surface. But there is an important sense in which appearances count for the good reason that someone's style is indicative of their character.

After all, most would recognise that to be stylish is far harder than to be fashionable. This is because style can bring out something admirable within the person concerned. Edina in *Absolutely Fabulous* is fashionable. Nelson Mandela – not known for wearing fashionable clothes – has style. And we know who is the better human being. As a former editor of *Vogue* put it: 'Fashion can be bought. Style one must possess.'

However, it is hard to give style to one's character. Nietzsche argued that true stylishness only comes when all the different parts of someone's character have been knitted together into a coherent whole. Think again of Mandela. His twenty-seven years on Robben Island could have left him ruined by anger or bitterness, literally a broken man. Yet he had the strength of character to overcome such fragmentation

– to put his life back together again. Remarkably, he is at ease with himself and the world. He is comfortable in his own skin, and clothes. His character shines through. This is the source of his style.

Oscar Wilde captured this point with another piece of wit. 'One should either be a work of art, or wear a work of art' – adding the second clause in recognition of how difficult it is for most to be stylish from within.

What not to say

The reason why it is so tricky to comment negatively on what someone chooses to wear is that this implies a criticism not just of what they look like but of who they are in themselves. In particular, it suggests that they lack style, and therefore perhaps character.

The good news, though, is that clothes can go a long way to making up any deficit. Better yet, some would say that clothes themselves are actually character-building. Think of what it does for an otherwise lost youth when he dons a military uniform. Or a young woman when she becomes a nurse. Again, to quote Wilde: 'A well-tied tie is the first serious step in life.'

So take courage from Virginia Woolf. 'There is much to support the view that it is clothes that wear us and not we them; we may make them take the mould of arm or breast, but they would mould our hearts, our brains, our tongues to their liking.'

Taking drugs

'Opium had long ceased to found its empire on spells of pleasure; it was solely by the tortures connected with the attempt to abjure it that it kept its hold.'   Thomas De Quincey

What might be said

There is little point in rehearsing the risks of taking drugs. They are well known, especially perhaps by those who take them. Cigarette packets with their ominous warnings are like miniature versions of the stone tablets on which the commandments were written, and about as effective. Neither is philosophy going to persuade addicts to come off.

No, the aim here is to ask whether it is possible to conceive of a life of pleasure that does not necessitate flirting with oblivion, temporary or permanent. Or rather, to put the case that hedonism is one of the notions most commonly misunderstood by the very people who would call themselves hedonistic. It's not an easy sell: the ancient philosophers who understood it correctly also understood that pleasure is hard work. The struggle is to resist the easy nod to more drugs, and opt for more of life.

There is a scene in Danny Boyle's film *Trainspotting* that stands out for me. Mark Renton has come off heroin and been through the nausea and cravings of cold turkey. Once he is able to leave his room, his mother takes him on the first outing of his new life – to the social club. And, Bingo! She has been marking his card and spots that he has won. 'House! House!' she shouts to the caller with delight. You know she will go over the moment with her friends for weeks.

Renton, though, barely notices. He doesn't speak. Even the winnings, subsequently counted out in front of him, don't stir him. The camera pans back, taking in the whole room; he is sitting in frozen insensibility amidst a sea of excitement. His voice bleakly narrates: 'Once the pain goes away, that's when the real battle starts. Depression. Boredom. You feel so fucking low, you'll want to fucking top yourself.'

The question is not just whether anything can ever feel pleasurable again after the 'just, subtle and mighty opium', that, as De Quincey put it in the high days of his addiction, apparently held the keys to paradise. It is whether anything can colour bourgeois world-weariness at all?

What is at stake

Epicurus was famous for his philosophy of pleasure during his own lifetime, the second half of the fourth and the first half of the third centuries BCE. He was also often wildly misunderstood. Enemies spread rumours that he vomited twice a day from indulgence, that he was so fat he couldn't rise from his chair, and that he accused others of pushing drugs – a sure sign of depravity.

Luckily, he also had many friends to defend him, and to pass his true thoughts on. They insisted that he was content with plain bread and water. Or that he was often heard to say: 'Send me a little pot of cheese, that, when I like, I may fare sumptuously.' In fact, he despaired of people who strive incessantly for paltry things and declared it futile to seek limitless pleasure, not least because the capacities that nature has given us for pleasure are themselves limited. He was an early advocate of the law of diminishing returns. However, Epicurus was not an ascetic, and did not believe that self-denial was the path to happiness.

To understand what he was really driving at it is necessary to unpack his concept of hedonism. He was a hedonist, in the sense that he thought that 'pleasure is the starting-point and goal of living happily', as he wrote to his friend Menoeceus. However, his hedonism was not one that advocated the continual indulgence and intensification of pleasure, as perhaps the modern, colloquial use of the term implies. Rather, Epicurean hedonism is about accepting one's lot and finding pleasure in that. It is about cultivating an attitude that enjoys what one has, even if it is only bread and water, as opposed to despising meagre food because a feast would be better.

This, then, is the first lesson for the serious pleasure-seeker: learn to take pleasure in what it is possible for you to have. To seek pleasure in what you lack is to gain the pain of insatiable longing.

But, the modern hedonist might reply: in periods of plenty, such as ours today, there is no need to subsist on bread and water. Pleasures abound: eat, drink and be merry because you can! Ah, replies Epicurus, that way lies pain too.

His hedonism was derived from studying the psychology of pleasure. He noticed that people routinely fall into cycles of greed when desires can be fed unchecked. Cities, he thought, are places that particularly nurture this craving. When many people live in close proximity wealth becomes a relative thing, because those who have enough are constantly tempted to envy those who have more. 'Nothing is enough to someone for whom enough is little,' he mused.

Incidentally, he thought a similar risk attends a certain kind of philosophy, the sort that dreams of a time when everything will be understood. Such seduction by grandiose goals only causes distraction in the souls of men since it is a desire for the impossible. One of his doctrines ran: 'Natural wealth is both limited and easy to acquire, but wealth as defined by groundless opinions extends without limits.'

This is the second lesson: you need to educate your capacity for pleasure. Do not be fooled into thinking that pleasure is a quantitative thing, as if more is always better. Rather, it is quality that counts. Epicurus' was a hedonism of appreciation, not accumulation; of the gourmet, not the gorger.

And this leads to his third, most profound point. The test is not whether everyone has the capacity to become a Heston Blumenthal, though there is much to be said for educating the palate. The test is whether they are able to be themselves.

The point about being yourself is that your pleasures then serve to enhance the person you are – they make you more you; as opposed to those pleasures that are really a means of escaping yourself, most obviously so in the taking of drugs. Such dubious pleasures do not build someone up. They break them down.

This is what Thomas De Quincey came to loathe about his addiction more than anything: his inability to be himself.

> The opium-eater loses none of his moral sensibilities or aspirations. He wishes and longs as earnestly as ever to realise what he believes possible, and feels to be exacted by duty; but his intellectual apprehension of what is possible infinitely outruns his power, not of execution only, but even of power to attempt. He lies under the weight of incubus and nightmare; he lies in sight of all that he would fain perform, just as a man forcibly confined to his bed by the mortal languor of a relaxing disease, who is compelled to witness injury or outrage offered to some object of his tenderest love: he curses the spells which chain him down from motion; he would lay down his life if he might but get up and walk; but he is powerless as an infant, and cannot even attempt to rise.

What not to say

Recreational drugs are very much part of the logic of late capitalism. Happiness is conceived in terms of possessions, pleasure in terms of more. Oliver James, the psychologist, has given a name to this complex: affluenza. In his book of the same title it is described as a virus of depression, anxiety, addiction and ennui. Drugs make absolute sense in this world, since they are both the supposed antidote to depression, anxiety and ennui, and simultaneously pander to the addiction tendency.

Epicurus' message is simple: less is more. But in opting for less – quality not quantity – you have to fight against the character of the age. This is why it can be so hard to conceive of a life of pleasure, let alone live it, that does not necessitate, at least from time to time, flirting with oblivion – temporary or for ever.

Going on holiday

'A perpetual holiday is a good working definition of hell.'

George Bernard Shaw

What might be said

There is only one thing guaranteed to cause more hedging and ducking than asking a friend whether you can go on holiday with them. And that is another friend asking whether they can go on holiday with you. Everyone knows that when you go on holiday you cannot escape yourself. Well, why compound the problem by making it impossible to escape your friends too?

And yet sometimes it has to happen. Your partner may not fancy altitude sickness on the Tibetan plateau. The tedium of the beach may have caused the break-up of your last relationship and now you are single. You cannot face the loneliness of eating dinner on your own. You must ask a friend. Who, then, and how?

He felt abandoned, outcast. He regarded himself as highly sociable, and only required of his friends that they be human. But they had made themselves strangers – a source of pain not pleasure. Now he is on what is effectively an enforced solitary holiday. And yet, with this melancholy comes an opportunity. Aloneness allows him to ask himself, what am I?

This situation is the one that the eighteenth-century philosopher Jean-Jacques Rousseau found himself in when he began his *Reveries of a Solitary Walker*. The book was written in the last years of his life when he had come to the realisation that much of it had been spent in a fevered search for truth and freedom, battling opponents and himself. Lately, though, he had found the peace of mind that comes with knowing nothing worse can befall him. It seems a dark sort of tranquillity, though it is less shadowy for the remembrance of delightful times and the fascination of giving an account of himself.

He remembers an earlier holiday when he was also alone. It lasted about two months, and was spent on the Island of Saint-Pierre, in Lake Bienne, Switzerland. Unknown to travellers, and supporting only one house, it was a paradise for those ready to 'drink deeply of the beauty of nature and to meditate in a silence which is unbroken but for the cry of eagles, the occasional song of birds and the roar of streams cascading down from the mountains'.

The break came after a very bad personal incident and, in stark contrast, turned out to be the happiest time of Rousseau's life. So what was the key to his unexpected contentment? Idleness – a sudden ability to do nothing. He could not have planned it that way; it was in escaping the bad incident that he unwittingly arrived unaccompanied and empty-handed. Papers were replaced by flowers, books by grasses, literary conversations by nature trails. The exercise, the singleness and the beauty were together an elixir – though like the philosopher's stone, the magic ingredient seemed more than these elements alone could add up to.

Which is why, looking back, his perfect holiday conjured up ambivalent feelings. 'I should like to know what there was in it that was attractive enough to give me such deep, tender and lasting regrets that even fifteen years later I am incapable of thinking of this beloved place without being overcome by pangs of longing.'

Perhaps the risk of holidaying on his own allowed him a rare glimpse of the ultimate mystery – existence as it is in itself.

What is at stake

The reason vacationing with a friend is so risky is the stress. Holidays are only patchily relaxing. Holiday-makers are often as tense as an arachnophobic in the Invertebrate House at London Zoo, and as irascible as an atheist reading *The Lives of the Saints.* You know your family as tourists – that on holiday they have an even vaguer idea of time-keeping than you and less desire to do the sights. But your apparently easy-going friend could turn into a check-list Nazi, or souvenir obsessive, as a traveller. Or they might come loaded with camera equipment. You had assumed that they would enjoy the quiet contemplation of a view, like you. There was no indication, ahead of time, that every scene would be viewed as a challenge to outdo an award-winning nature programme.

The strangeness of friends abroad is one matter, but

further things are at stake too, for holidays are strewn with hopes that are complicated by the presence of friends.

Just consider the word: 'travel' comes from the French, 'travail'. Since holidays almost always involve travelling, the modern holiday-maker is desperate to ensure they gain a decent return for their hard work. After all, they have had to plan, save, pack and brave the airport – which, as Dennis Potter commented, is the place that embodies the meaning of the phrase 'terminal illness'. On top of all that, who wants the added concern of whether their friend is having a good time too?

In fact, by making travel a consumer product, tourism has exacerbated the sense of injustice should imperfections creep into the experience. The package holiday was originally envisaged as luxury at a discount for lower-income families. It has become a straightforward offer of low-life, as anyone who has had to sit next to a teenager consuming miniatures on a charter flight to the Mediterranean will know. Which scrimping friend was it who booked that flight for us?

Paradoxically, it may be when the travel company fails to provide everyday things, not the promised novelties, that the greatest upset occurs. I once heard a man bitterly complaining that there was no soap, which seemed incongruous given that the holiday was hiking through the hills of north Thailand, over-nighting in jungle shacks. But the soap was not, of course, his fundamental problem. Rather it was resentment at being compelled to go on the holiday to start with, to accompany his friend.

Friends may compromise other hopes that make for a good time away. There can be the desire to gain some new experience. The traveller may want to improve or test themselves – in the discovery of an exotic culture, the indulgence of an extreme sport, or the reading of a lengthy canonical tome. How irritating, then, are the friends who laugh at your pretensions or sneer at your fun. They turn out to be those whom Horace had in mind when he noted: 'They change their clime, not their frame of mind, who rush across the sea.' Such mono-modes imprison you in the rut of normal life. They starve the holiday of its freedom. If a change is as good as a rest, by disallowing change they may ruin your relaxation.

Another final caution is worth airing: the trials of going on holiday with a couple when you yourself are single. Anyone who finds themselves in such a situation rapidly realises that they are on the wrong end of a systematic injustice. Couples always make decisions *à deux*. Even when they cannot agree, their disagreement becomes the main deliberation. The single person is invariably outvoted. It's in the numbers. They allow no other outcome. You only have at best one third of the papers. And woe betide you if a row between them requires you to exercise a casting vote.

What not to say

The Chinese writer Lin Yutang has written: 'A good traveller is one who does not know where he is going to, and a perfect traveller does not know where he came from.' I have, in fact, been on very good holidays with friends. And in retrospect, those friends were ones who fitted Yutang's description.

It may not seem very flattering – people who feel

themselves to be strangers in a foreign land. But that is an invaluable character trait to have when travelling. Such people do not impose their own agenda. They do not pack their psychological baggage along with their T-shirts and shades. They will not compound your problems, and may even lighten your load.

Losing your job

'All that matters is love and work.'   Sigmund Freud

What might be said

Losing your job routinely appears in the list of the top five most stressful things in life: above 'moving house', below 'death of a child', about the same as 'end of a marriage'. According to the so-called science of happiness, becoming unemployed is equivalent to a loss of income at least a third higher than the actual financial loss of being sacked. Worse, people in employment suffer from an indirect effect – a persistent fear of being asked, one day, to clear their desk. Few concerns in modern society can match unemployment's ability to slash our well-being.

Little wonder that it is so hard to talk about. When someone loses their job, offering sympathy feels like rubbing salt into the wound. In reply, what can they say except to vocalise this terrible thing that has happened to them, again. Rising unemployment is a social curse, or a price that unlucky souls have to pay for the sake of society as a whole, as if people being laid off were a kind of leeching. 'Unemployed youth' is a euphemism for 'unsociable behaviour'.

And if you know someone who has been made redundant, there are the weeks and months when you have to encourage them about new ads or applications. It is uncomfortable to do so because it appears to underline their passivity, their marginality in the capitalist system; they are 'economically inactive', net takers not contributors. 'Something will come along,' we say because something – anything – is better than nothing.

Mr Phillips, fifty, is middle-class, an accountant, married to Mrs Phillips, lives underneath the Heathrow flight path and – as if inhabiting his own worst nightmare – is out of a job.

However, on the first Monday of his unemployment, he leaves his house as usual. And walks – 'outside the shell of a normal day' as the author of the eponymous novel, John Lancaster, has put it.

Whilst obsessively calculating the costs and probabilities of virtually everything around him – the old habits of the office being maintained to facilitate his denial of the dominant yet unintelligible fact of his new existence – he stumbles across a bank robbery, a rescue and a pornographer, all well beyond his bourgeois comprehension. They are experiences that exacerbate his inability to give an account of himself; he no longer has a narrative of his life.

The premise of the whole story is that Mr Phillips cannot tell Mrs Phillips what has happened to him, not because he cannot speak, but because he could not grasp the meaning of the words were he to utter them. He can no more communicate his unemployment to her than he could communicate it to the dog.

What is at stake

In a word: need. Or better, the need to be needed. Work not only ensures that your bank account has a positive balance, it is the chief means by which many people credit their lives with meaning too. In addition to cash, it supplies a frame of reference, dignity and a key resource for friendship. Work shapes your soul as much as your office suit clothes your body. We become what we are, Nietzsche observed.

Conversely, unemployment is a disaster because it destroys self-respect and social connection. And it is *being made* unemployed that is the curse. For the increasingly small group of people in society who have never needed to work, unemployment is no more distressing than 'missing' an episode of a soap that they have never previously watched.

There is an issue of gender to bear in mind here, inasmuch as unemployment might be thought more of a fear for men than women. It does seem to be the case that, although husbands and fathers, for example, might say their family and children are the most important things in their lives, they nevertheless think of their work as the way in which they most importantly fulfil that sense of responsibility. For many men, children and work are a double helix in the same virtuous spiral of commitment.

However, for women, working appears to be of growing importance. My grandmother would say as a matter of fact that when she married she stopped working because that was what women did. When looking back, though, she toyed with the thought that she could have been more stretched in her life had she done more than raise a family – not least because her daughters worked and loved it. Their daughters, in turn, never thought otherwise than to gain qualifications that could provide a career. Today, they are almost as likely to be the chief breadwinner as their husbands. And if they don't have paid employment, you do well to recognise the work they do at home. In two generations, 'housewife' has become a pejorative term.

What is going on in this change is, according to Hannah Arendt, the final stage in a transformation that reaches back to pre-industrial times. In *The Human Condition*, she draws an ancient distinction between labour and work. If we lived naturally, like our evolutionary cousins the chimps, we would labour, merely doing the things that are necessary to survive and reproduce. But we would not work. To work is to be in the world of meaning. It is like the difference between foraging for bananas and shopping for bananas: foraging is menial and unproductive because all it achieves is finding bananas; shopping, though, is productive because it contributes to the market economy, wealth generation and the social life of humankind. (More disturbingly, slaves were thought not to work but to labour, since they were doing what was deemed natural to them – as if they were, in effect, tame animals.)

So work underpins the world that is characteristic of human existence, in institutions like markets. It creates the sense of who we are as people. 'Work and its product, the human artifice, bestow a measure of permanence and durability upon the futility of mortal life and the fleeting character of human time,' Arendt says. In a sense, to work is to preserve and give birth to the world for those who will come after us – which explains the connection fathers feel between their work and providing for their children.

The distinction also helps to explain the attitudes that are held about different kinds of work. Farming, for example, holds a place of special dignity in the post-industrialised world of work, because to till the soil is to be close to the cycles of nature and yet is also to transform the raw stuff of the land into a valuable commodity for human society. Respect for this activity is what is meant whenever urbanites are told to value the life of the countryside, because of the service rural people perform in looking after the land.

Alternatively, think of the efforts that those with intellectual occupations make to demonstrate their usefulness to society at large. The value of their work is doubtful because it is not always clear how productive it is. Maybe these intellectuals are just pen-pushers, as people say when they speak ill of bureaucrats; or perhaps they should go and look for a 'real job', as others will routinely say of academics.

In short, productive work makes human beings and is the measure of human beings. To be unproductive or, worse, to have unproductivity thrust upon you – as when you lose your job – is, therefore, profoundly dehumanising.

What not to say

People's work defines who they are. Famously, Silicon Valley workers reply to the question, 'Where are you from?' with the answer: 'Oracle' or 'Sun' or 'Apple'. Alternatively, work shapes people's lives. At a mundane level, they dress up in work clothes. At a deeper level, their company or trade informs their character by its own pervasive culture: accountants, builders, actors – these words not only name a job but describe a kind of person. And most profoundly of all, work can implicitly be taken as the justification for an individual's place in society. It is the way in which they contribute, the way they are productive.

Conversely, with the loss of a job can go dignity, self-sufficiency and self-esteem. Those who don't or can't work are vulnerable to accusations of sponging.

So if a sense of identity is perhaps the greatest benefit of work, it can be devastating when you lose your job. The need to work becomes a huge burden for the unemployed individual. If you ask someone, 'What do you do?' – meaning who are you – and the answer is 'nothing', the implication is that they are a no one. What not to say? 'What do you do?'

Making money

What might be said

It is said that money talks, meaning that it buys influence. Bob Dylan sang that it doesn't talk, it swears, meaning that it is obscene. Well, I would say that money – big money – neither talks nor swears but screams.

It screams in the sense that if you are near someone who has lots of money it is very hard to hear what they are saying. The one fact about them, their high net worth, speaks louder than any words. It speaks so loudly that even what their wealth might mean is hard to discern. Privilege? Power? Possibilities?

I remember the first time I interviewed a billionaire. I struggled over what to use as an ice-breaker. 'Nice hotel?' – it was only the smartest in London. 'Do you know the city?' – know it, he owned a fair chunk of it. I decided to ask whether his work ever allowed him time for a holiday. It did, so many in fact that he and his wife had run out of places to go. That year they were being flown to Antarctica.

Billionaires, like gods, do not often linger with mortals. But perhaps a more common difficulty over what to say when confronted by serious cash occurs when a friend joins the lesser, but still impressive, collective of millionaires. When one person makes far more cash than another, the income disparity can be a serious challenge to the friendship. Another trio of possible reactions raise their ugly heads and can be very hard to ignore. Jealousy. Sycophancy. A sense of injustice. Friendship has few defences against these.

I was taking a short flight on one of the so-called no-frills airlines. I say 'so-called' because these flights are actually full of frills, it is just that you have to pay extra for them. That is fair enough when it comes to buying snacks, but in the need to squeeze each passenger for profit, a great deal of effort is made during these flights to sell all kinds of things. The most annoying are scratch cards. The 'stunning' prizes from these lottery tickets are trumpeted across the cabin by the member of the crew who fancies that a camp impersonation of the already too camp Dale Winton will be endlessly amusing to those on board.

On this particular flight, I had done my best to ignore the noise of the hard sell, and had presumably done pretty well, since the first thing I remember about the incident was another crew-member running down the cabin shouting at his colleagues: 'Five hundred pounds! Someone has won five hundred pounds!' Then, a few seconds later, a ripple of applause spread out to fill almost the whole cabin.

I was bemused: why was everyone, or almost everyone, clapping? The mood of the outburst felt like joy, as might happen if we had been told we were finally landing after a long delay. But that couldn't be quite right, since there was no collective gain from one person's winnings. Perhaps, the round of applause was one of congratulation, hyped up by the excited air steward? But I didn't think that was correct either, since all the lucky person had done was scratch a card.

Then I thought I had it. The clapping was for the luck that this lucky person had found. Sometimes, it is said, people make their luck. In such cases, there is no reason to clap since they have put in the effort to make the luck, as it were. This guy, though, had done nothing. 'There is much good luck in the world, but it is luck,' wrote E. M. Forster – and this person had it.

And there was something else. He was lucky with money. It is said that we live in a meritocratic world, though this is not strictly true, since the people with serious money – like the owners of the no-frills airlines – have proportionately far more money than their merit alone can justify. So it was as if, on that plane, a veil had been lifted and the goddess Fortuna herself had been present; it was only £500, but it gave us a taste of something that is the preserve of the very few: to suddenly, *ex nihilo*, land extraordinary amounts of money.

What is at stake

To think about this issue, let us turn it on its head. Let us imagine that we are one of the rich ones. This has the advantage of avoiding what is probably only possible for the saints: not begrudging the wealthy their money. Even Adam Smith, hardly the enemy of affluence, could sound surly on the matter. 'The chief enjoyment of riches consists in the parade of riches,' he wrote with at least mild bitterness.

Niccolò Machiavelli is an illuminating guide for this exercise. The author of *The Prince*, a book that could be subtitled *Kingship for Dummies*, was not a prince himself. It was written to win the favour of a prince, namely Lorenzo de' Medici, the Magnificent. What is notable about this is that Machiavelli had suffered cruelly at the hands of regal tyrants. So his book was a remarkable exercise in empathy too. It was even perhaps a therapy, to come to terms with his past misfortune, and might help those grappling with the matter of being less well off than they would like.

So the conceit is that you are rich, like a prince. And the central question is this: how should you be generous?

A chapter in *The Prince* called 'Generosity and Parsimony' provides the lead. Machiavelli begins with an obvious point: for the rich and powerful it is clearly desirable to have a generous reputation. However, Machiavelli immediately follows that thought with a piece of the political realism for which he is remembered. In order to be regarded as generous, you have to *earn* your reputation.

The conundrum here is that you cannot earn a reputation for generosity by being sincerely virtuous in your largesse – say, in the modern way, by making anonymous donations or high tax contributions – because people will not notice it. Concealing your generosity will lead them to presume you are parsimonious, for all that you might have given away millions. Rather, you have to make an ostentatious display of your charity, perhaps by calling in the press or lending endowments your name. This, though, in turn, ceases to seem like generosity and more like a calculated act to win praise or appease guilt. Moreover, unless you are as loaded as a Gates or Buffett, the chances are that in order to succeed you will have to be so lavish that you could end up giving away your whole fortune. Then, paradoxically, you are at risk of being despised. 'Why could you not have given some to me?' your friends will think if not say. It is unfair, but they could still end up branding you a miser. Machiavelli concludes: 'There is nothing so self-defeating as generosity: in the act of practising it, you lose the ability to do so, and you become either poor and despised or, seeking to escape poverty, rapacious and hated.'

But he has a solution to this that is twofold. First, be generous but in secret, targeting the causes for which you are passionate. Second, and simply, learn not to mind being thought a miser. It may not be pleasant, but Machiavelli thinks it is the only realistic option. After all, if you give away too much, in the vain attempt to be thought generous, you may end up with nothing left for your good causes.

Having said that, there is a chance that this cloud might have a silver lining; your acts of quiet generosity may pay dividends for your public persona in time. For generosity will alter your character; it will be made manifest, if subtly, in the person you are. Friends will say you are a generous soul, maybe without exactly realising why – which is even better. So whatever you decide to do, don't not give away anything at all.

What not to say

The exercise is over. You are not rich but yourself again, a person of modest means, but you have empathised with the dilemmas of the wealthy. So what would you say now?

The Bible says that of those to whom much has been

given, much will be required. Do you not have just a little more sympathy for them as they struggle with their fabulous lives and its burden?

Needing money

'Neither a borrower, nor a lender be.'   Shakespeare

What not to say

No one likes asking for money. Even if you have a good reason for doing so, perhaps wanting a friend to invest in a business for which they might receive some return, it feels risky and humiliating. It puts you in someone else's debt, financially and emotionally. It is like becoming a child again, and having to ask Daddy for money.

It is embarrassing to be asked for money too. It is awkward to have people who are indebted to you because they become beholden to you as well. A net of obligation is superimposed upon a relationship that was previously one of freely chosen commitments. As Shakespeare continues: 'For loan oft loses itself and a friend.'

Personally, I do not like it when people ask for money instead of gifts, say at a big birthday or wedding. It is impossible to decide how much to give because you have to engage in a calculus of how much the relationship is worth. A gift is different: it is a token of love or affection.

115

Money is not a symbol of anything. It is calculated, a measure.

> The aching humiliation of asking for money is wonderfully caught by Evelyn Waugh in *Brideshead Revisited*. It is the long vacation and Charles has returned from Oxford to stay at his father's house in London. He has no choice. He has no money. The summer looks bleak, unless he can conjure some cash from his father. He cannot raise the matter directly. It would suggest that he spent his allowance like a bookie, precisely as Sebastian had teased him. So, at dinner, he pretends idly to comment to his father that one of the 'problems' of the vacation is financial in nature.
>
> There then follows a hilarious verbal joust between the two, with only one rule: neither a borrower nor a lender be. Charles must not ask, because that would be to admit defeat; and his father must not offer, because that would bring an end to the battle.
>
> His father suggests he is too young to worry about 'a thing like that'. He really should not let money be his master. He advises that he is the worst person to come to, having never himself been 'in Queer Street' – his favourite euphemism for being cash-strapped. He recalls that Charles's cousin ended up in Australia following some ill-defined financial imprudence.
>
> In the end, Charles's father wins. But then he is the one with the money.

What is at stake

No philosopher can have analysed the power of money, or described it in such vivid language, as Karl Marx. It is central to his famous concept of alienation. Put simply, when something gains a price, its wider value becomes a poor, secondary consideration. One only has to think of the escalating sums exchanged for pieces of modern art to see this process in action. Their intrinsic worth is routinely doubted even by the artist. Conversely too: if money is the measure of worth, those without money feel worthless. To borrow from Oscar Wilde, this is the situation of knowing the price of everything and the value of nothing. Money alienates us from what gives meaning to life.

The root of the problem, according to Marx, is the business of being paid for what we do. Now, of course, being paid for working is a good thing, inasmuch as an income buys a standard of life. But when we receive cash for doing something, the satisfaction that we may find in what we have done is compromised, because our pleasure in our achievement is substituted by the pleasure of receiving money for doing it.

To put it another way, the system of being paid sets up a kind of scale. On one side of the balance is the satisfaction of the work itself; on the other is the satisfaction of receiving the financial reward for doing it. A humanly rewarding life is one in which the balance is tipped clearly in favour of doing the job well. An alienated life is one tipped the other way. The worst case would be someone who gets no pleasure from what they do and works solely for money.

Having said that, even those who enjoy their work cannot escape the effects of being paid for it. You might think that it is only someone who prefers money over everything who can be bought, but is not everyone who lives in a capitalist economy debauched to a degree, since everyone needs money? Everyone must sell their services to survive. The system would make hustlers of us all.

Marx deployed the pimping analogy to describe the predicament. In the *1844 Manuscripts*, he writes that producers – that is, anyone who works – are effectively forced to play the pimp between what they are selling and the person to whom they seek to sell their labour. 'Every product is a bait with which to seduce away the other's very being, his money,' Marx explains. We may work with the 'utmost amiability'. But whether acknowledged or not, everything we sell comes with a note that reads: 'Dear friend, I give you what you need, but you know the *conditio sine qua non*; you know the ink in which you have to sign yourself over to me; in providing for your pleasure, I fleece you.'

Now, taken literally, the idea that all human commerce is 'tainted love' might be thought an exaggeration. And yet that is what is so embarrassing about the situation in which someone asks directly for money. All is suddenly not as it seemed. Amiability is stretched to a limit. The blatant request strips away the bonhomie that usually detracts from the business of handling the filthy lucre. Without even the brown envelope of bureaucracy to conceal the exchange, its fundamentally debasing nature is laid bare. This is why asking for money feels shaming, embarrassing and dehumanising to all concerned. Marx's language then feels not only colourful but right.

Even if someone truly needs the money, because without it they will be in serious trouble, asking for it somehow casts aspersions on their character. Perhaps they do not have the prudence to live within their means. Perhaps they are spongers. Perhaps the skills they sell to make a living are not worth very much – maybe, according to the logic of money, *they* are not worth very much. Jonathan Wolff, in his book *Why Read Marx Today?*, puts it well: 'Need is natural to human beings, and the human world depends entirely on people taking steps to satisfy each others' needs. Yet, Marx says, under capitalism the language of needs is debased. It becomes humiliating to ask for something on the basis that you need it; it becomes imploring, or whining.'

What not to say

I think there is only one response that is possibly risk-free if someone asks for money, or if you must ask. Give, or ask for it, as a gift. Not for interest. Or for it to be paid back. To insist on either of these is to be obliged to one another – not as parents are to their children, or husbands are to their wives, but as bank managers are to their clients. In the realm of human relationships, as opposed to commercial agreements, if you cannot be generous, or you suspect that the person you might ask cannot be so, then neither give nor receive.

In fact, even an exchange as a gift is a risk. Say a friend does give some money to you. You are grateful, but therein lies the rub. For you now owe them a debt of gratitude. In other words, in receiving the gift you are put in their debt almost as squarely as if they had charged! Moreover, they are entitled to feel pleased with themselves on account of their generosity. So, in giving, they receive something: self-congratulation.

In short, the giver receives; the receiver gives. It is more blessed to give than to receive. As the French philosopher Jacques Derrida put it, 'A gift is something that you cannot be thankful for.'

Work–life balance

'All work and no play makes Jack a dull boy.'
Seventeenth-century proverb

What might be said

To be anxious about the balance between time spent working and time spent with family is a very twenty-first-century neurosis. The idea that the working classes might be on the threshold of a new life – the charmed one, long enjoyed by the moneyed aristocrat – has its origins in the industrial revolution. The march of the machines was supposed to automate manual jobs, freeing the worker to labour less, without jeopardising the capacity of capital to grow more. It was a pipe dream put paid to by the computer; the ultimate productivity tool, as manufacturers like to call the PC, has automated tasks by the shovelful, and yet only created more work in its wake. So we must now proactively address our work–life balance and consciously arrive at a choice between our career and the care of ourselves.

These days, many managers are amenable to employees requesting flexi-time, part-time hours, and sabbaticals.

Although the pressure is on to stay competitive, much of the shame has gone from asking to work less. Progressive companies may think of their staff as stakeholders, and want to please them as much as their customers. However, there is a new, more radical way of tackling work–life imbalance, with which people might catch you out. They do not want to work less. They want to up sticks, move away and forsake the rat race entirely.

This can leave you not knowing quite what to say, since it implicitly challenges your lifestyle. If they are downsizing, leaving the city for the country, and changing a highly paid job for something more humanly rewarding, then the implication might be that greed and fripperies are what actually rule *your* life. Or, if they are going to join one of the burgeoning number of communities that seek to lead lives at least one step back from unbridled consumerism, then you might start to question your own pursuit of happiness. After all, given that most people in the West have more than enough to live on, what is it about work that is so addictive?

It happened to me about four years ago. He is one of my closest friends. We both worked freelance – myself as a writer, he as an artist – and I assumed that he, like me, felt that a life free of office hours brought freedoms enough. We could meet for lunch more or less as we chose, take time off without counting down holiday entitlements, and work hard, not only for money but because we had managed to carve out jobs that offered vocational fulfilment.

Then, one summer, he and his partner went looking for a house in France. It was supposed to be a holiday home, but the next I heard of it they had found an ideal property and were not only buying it but moving into it. Later my friend told me the full story. He had become deeply depressed with the relentless pace of life in London. He was weary of the low-level aggression he met daily on the bus. He was sick of the cash-cow economy that, vampire-like, drains your money as fast as you can supply it. He wanted space, a calmer pattern of life, quiet.

Four years on, his new life is a blessing and a success. Four years on, I am still tinkering with my work–life balance.

What is at stake

The philosopher Herbert Marcuse wrote *Eros and Civilisation* in the 1950s. It inspired many of the countercultural social movements of the 1960s. However, that is not to say it can now be dismissed as a hippy tract of yesteryear. If anything, it was prophetic in the way it describes the battle between work and leisure that is fought to this day.

The 'Eros' of his title is borrowed from Freud: it is the pleasure principle, in the sense of the energy that we enjoy expending in leisure, pleasure and sex. The 'Civilisation' of the title is what you might think: it is the culture and community that, in its capitalist guise, supply us with the goods and services we value. However, Marcuse's sense of civilisation is also a form of consciousness, one that tells us we should be productive and obedient, in order to advance civilisation and stay civilised. He sums this consciousness up in what he calls the 'performance principle'.

The performance principle reaches into every part of

civilised life. It is not just characteristic of the workplace. It catches us at a young age, teaching us the value of education and efficiency in pre-school learning. It shapes our leisure lives too, for fear that if we were to taste freedom and overindulge the pleasure principle, we might undermine civilisation. Marcuse explains how:

> The goods and services that the individuals buy control their needs and petrify their faculties. In exchange for the commodities that enrich their life, the individuals sell not only their labour but also their free time. The better living is off-set by the all-pervasive control over living. People dwell in apartment concentrations – and have private automobiles with which they can no longer escape into a different world. They have huge refrigerators filled with frozen food. They have dozens of newspapers and magazines that espouse the same ideals. They have innumerable choices, innumerable gadgets which are all of the same sort and keep them occupied and divert their attention from the real issue – which is the awareness that they could both work less and determine their own needs and satisfactions.

In another section he offers a sophisticated version of what everyone who works has experienced at least from time to time, the feeling of being too exhausted at the end of the day to do anything but crash: '[Civilised man] has to work in order to live, and this work requires not only eight, ten, twelve daily hours of his time and therefore a corresponding diversion of energy, but also during these hours and the remaining ones a behaviour in conformity with the standards and morals of the performance principle.'

In other words, the performance principle is at odds

with the pleasure principle. And what civilisation means is the repression of freely determined leisure. This carries a dark side. 'The individual pays by sacrificing his time, his consciousness, his dreams; civilisation pays by sacrificing its own promises of liberty, justice and peace for all,' Marcuse continues. However, this is something that the vast majority of people agree to, or at least conform to, because of the perceived benefits of civilisation – the apartments, cars, fridges and, above all, the choice.

Marcuse's picture of the forces that shape us, internally and externally, is compelling because of its explanatory power. For example, it can account for the tremendous guilt people feel when they sense that they are 'indulging' themselves in 'too much' leisure. Such behaviour is perceived as a crime 'against the wise order which secures the goods and services for the progressive satisfaction of human needs'.

It also shows why technology does not free up time for leisure but actually generates more work. 'Civilisation has to defend itself against the spectre of a world which could be free. If society cannot use its growing productivity for reducing repression (because such usage would upset the hierarchy of the status quo), productivity must be turned against the individuals; it becomes itself an instrument of universal control.' Like an army, people have to be kept in a permanent state of productive mobilisation. Pleasure must not compromise the performance of the workers.

What not to say

The person who wants to downsize and opt out is, therefore, engaged in a highly subversive act. At a social level, they can be perceived as a threat to everything that drives progress. This is why, for example, successive governments grow more and more alarmed at the number of people who move to live abroad, seeking a better quality of life. It is not just that they threaten the labour markets. They also seem to challenge national values.

At a personal level, those people who opt for a more radical readjustment to their work–life balance are a threat too (and we secretly hope that they will not find their dream but will soon be back, contrite, chastened and ready to rejoin hard-working civilisation).

But if they do, don't say, 'I told you so.' For their failure would be yours too. 'We are closer to the ants than to the butterflies. Very few people can endure much leisure,' wrote Gerald Brenan. The performance principle would make ants of us all.

Does he take sugar?

'Who is going to want to read about a fifteen-year-old kid with a disability living in Swindon with his father?' Mark Haddon – author of the best-selling novel, *The Curious Incident of the Dog in the Night-Time* – about a fifteen-year-old kid with a disability living in Swindon with his father.

What might be said

The question, 'Does he take sugar?', has come to symbolise the way people can talk over the heads of those with a disability in a way that reveals their prejudice and misconceptions. They may be awkward with someone who is blind, not knowing quite how to communicate; uncomfortable with a handicapped child, wondering how they would cope if the responsibility was theirs; or fearful of someone with motor-neuron disease, thinking their slurred speech is a mental deficiency – and forgetting that this is the disability with which no less an intellectual than Professor Stephen Hawking lives. In their confusion, they almost forget that there is another human being in front of them.

Even when able-bodied people talk directly to the

disabled they might be patronising. It is a bit like the experience my grandmother had when she became old and frail. She told me that people make comments to you that you'd think were reserved for children. 'Oh, you are doing well,' they'd exclaim. Or, for the umpteenth time, 'How are you today?' Really, such comments conceal their inability to find the right thing to say.

It might be thought that prejudice against disabled people was lessening in modern society, perhaps as a result of equal opportunities legislation or greater medical understanding. However, the British Social Attitudes survey shows that, at least in the UK, there is still widespread prejudice.

In particular, people show distinct signs of unease at the thought of coming into contact with the disabled. According to the 2007 survey, 71 per cent of people interviewed said they would be less than comfortable if someone with schizophrenia moved in next door. And 79 per cent admitted the same disquiet at the thought of a close relative marrying someone with a condition like MS or severe arthritis. Only half say they would be very comfortable if a relative married a blind person.

The thing that makes the greatest difference to people's attitudes is knowing someone with a disability. The uneasiness around disability then rapidly falls away.

What is at stake

There are many ways to think through the prejudice against the disabled. A philosophical reflection on what it means perhaps has a certain freshness because of its novelty, and that freshness might be valuable if it cast disability in a different light.

The philosophical question begins with what counts as disability. Think of someone who is in a car crash and loses the use of their legs as a result. We would say that they are now disabled because it is clear that they could once walk and now cannot. However, for people born with a disability, being described as disabled can be objectionable because they have not lost a particular capacity; they simply never had it. It seems better in this case not to say that a disability is something that a person has. Rather it is another way of being.

There is also an implication in careless talk about disability that there is an ideal form of what it is to be human, from which the disabled fall short. The dangerous corollary of this is the implication that they are somehow less than human. Putting the morality of such an opinion to one side, it is flawed at a purely rational level. For example, physical variations exist across all individuals. Speaking personally, I am very short-sighted. If I lived in a world without contact lenses, laser eye-surgery or glasses I would be severely restricted in how I could function. But I do not, as a result, consider myself disabled.

Why not? It might be countered that I can overcome my 'disability' by wearing glasses. However, this opens up another difficulty in identifying what is a disability and what is merely a physical variation. It suggests a scale of disabilities: myopia and other conditions that can be rectified would be at one end; disabilities that mean life is ultimately not viable would be at another. But these are the easy cases – you rapidly get into all sorts of difficulty when trying to place others. And even short-sightedness eludes strict classification: if I wanted to play rugby or be a pilot, my poor eyesight, even with glasses, would become a severe disability again.

Then there is another issue. Many disabilities arise more from conditions within society than from the actual physical or mental difference itself. This becomes particularly clear with certain mental disabilities such as dyslexia. At school, where verbal and mathematical skills are rewarded, dyslexia might be thought a disability, but in business it may not matter at all, as many successful business leaders with dyslexia have shown.

Worse, being labelled disabled at one stage in life may itself become an impediment. Or, as the Canadian wheelchair-user Rick Hansen has written, 'My disability is that I cannot use my legs. My handicap is your negative perception of that disability, and thus of me.' His point is both that his wheelchair use becomes a problem because of the way society tends to provide access to buildings and vehicles, as if things could not be any other way, and also that people then see him as diminished, pitiful or abnormal because he is disabled.

Perhaps the handicap that the world places on Rick Hansen is intensified by our ever greater, and ever more perverse, idealisation of the human body – from the size zero model on the catwalk to the artificially sculpted beefcake at the gym. In fact, both these ideals may be disabled – the size zero girl by anorexia, the beefcake perhaps by impotence.

What not to say

The reason for exploring disability in this way is not to make some kind of politically correct point, as if the word itself should not be used. It is rather to open up just what is meant by disability and the prejudices that can be concealed within it. Again, the classic case of this is when disabled people are dehumanised and treated as being unable to answer for themselves. Over their heads, it is asked whether 'they' take sugar.

In other words, someone else's disability is quite likely to be your problem more than it is theirs.

Moving home

'Be it ever so humble, there's no place like home.'

A tortoise in Aesop's fable

What might be said

Mobility is celebrated as a precious manifestation of freedom. Cars, cell phones, credit cards, passports – many of people's most important possessions are predicated upon a way of life that values being on the move. So it is surprising that it can be so devastating when friends announce that they are moving. After all, relocating is only to be expected when people routinely travel for work and pleasure.

It is sad because you are left behind. Perhaps they are sad too because they will miss you and have to seek out new friends. It can be hard to know what to say because, whilst wanting to wish them well, you also wish they would stay. Perhaps they are moving for a better paid job; is money more important than your friendship, you might want to ask? Perhaps they are moving to sunnier climes; is that worth more than the warmth of your affection? And then there is the thought that maybe it is.

For the tortoise in Aesop's fable, having a mobile home – a shell – was a curse. Zeus had invited all the animals to his wedding. All showed up, apart from the tortoise, who excused herself, saying: 'Be it ever so humble, there's no place like home.' Zeus was furious and, thereafter, ordered the tortoise to carry her home with her wherever she went.

There is evidence that mobility is a curse as well as a blessing in the twenty-first century too. According to some recent research, a quarter of all Americans do not have anyone close with whom to talk. The scattering of friends and family across the continent and around the globe is a key cause of this loneliness. Similarly, in London, two fifths of people report that they have lost touch with former close friends. Relationship drift seems inherent to the transitoriness of urban life. Conversely, people who live the more settled life of the Scottish borders report fewer intimacy problems.

The internet can help people stay in touch, but nurturing a deeper trust seems to require a prior relationship with reserves of 'face-time'. For this reason, I think it is a fascinating development that avatars in Second Life seek to buy a place in virtual space if they can. I wonder whether the people behind them will, in time, come to think that close relationships cannot be place-independent. In the meantime, if email is presented to you as the medium through which your friendship is now to be continued, you are not wrong to feel betrayed. Hanging out online is a thin substitute for hanging out in the pub, playground or on the patio.

When I was a priest in the Church of England, I worked in the parish of St Cuthbert's, Billingham, an old village that had been consumed by the industrial sprawl of Teesside in the north-east of England. I moved up north for the job from Oxford. I had never lived anywhere for longer than three years and thought nothing of settling into a new place for new work.

Soon after my arrival, I visited an elderly husband and wife and asked them whether they had any children. 'Oh, he moved away,' I was told in a sad tone of voice. I imagined that their son had emigrated to Australia, so I asked how often they see him – perhaps once a year? 'Oh no, about once a week,' came the reply.

It turned out that their son had moved about three miles away, to Norton, across the A19. To his parents, with their deep ties to Billingham, it was another world.

What is at stake

In 1632, Galileo Galilei made his famous recantation. He had proved that the earth moved around the sun, and yet the opinion of the Inquisition proved as immovable as the planet that it believed to be the fixed centre of the universe. That Galileo later uttered the words 'but it does move' only serves to underline this famous incident in the history of science and religion. Galileo's trial became a cause célèbre.

However, in some ways his heliocentrism was the lesser part of the revolution he ignited. It was, after all, not a discovery but a rediscovery: the ancient Greeks knew as much. More profound were the implications of his work on the nature of space itself. For in Galileo's universe, space became infinite and undifferentiated. Afterwards, where a body is absolutely located became irrelevant; it is its relative position to other bodies that counts. As Michel Foucault reflected: 'In such a space the place of the Middle Ages turned out to be dissolved, as it were; a thing's place was no longer anything but a point in its movement.'

Foucault must have remembered Nietzsche's frightening reflection on the disorientation and alienation that stemmed from Galileo's untying of the celestial spheres: 'What were we doing when we unchained this earth from its sun? Whither is it moving now? Whither are we moving? Away from all suns? Are we not plunging continually? Backward, sideward, forward, in all directions? Is there still any up or down? Are we not straying as through an infinite nothing? Do we not feel the breath of empty space?'

Galileo, in effect, redefined place as no more or less than a portion of space. The move carried implications not just for science but for humanity's view of itself. In the same way that the new cosmology depicted the earth as free to move about the universe, as it were, human beings in subsequent centuries came to feel that the freedom to move about the earth was integral to their own liberation. A particular locale became a detail; a fixed place in society, an oppression. Today, enabled by post-industrial technologies of travel, anyone with minimal financial means can leave the place of their birth and set up home wherever they choose.

This is part of the 'demise of place', as John Inge has called it in his book *A Christian Theology of Place*. He shows that the precedence given to space, as opposed to place – and the former's associations with freedom, the latter's with constraint – has a long history. It reaches back to Aristotle, who defined place as a container for the space within which things happen. This took on explicitly negative connotations in neo-Platonic thought, which celebrated the idea of a transcendent soul that would throw off the limitations of its embodied place in the world after death. Place is about limits and boundaries. Space is about limitless possibilities. 'So it does not really matter whether I live in Glasgow or Beijing, and what kind of buildings surround me will have no significant effect on me,' writes Inge. Dreams of flying away are much more preferable.

However, whilst being able to move at will from place to place – in open space – is a tremendous good, it comes at a tremendous price. If we can be anywhere, then we might belong nowhere. A freedom to up sticks implies a difficulty with downing roots. If, as Nietzsche observed, we have become uncoupled from the sun, then maybe we have also become unhinged from ourselves.

Similarly, if being tied to a particular place is thought of as a burden, being embodied might be regarded as a curse – for our bodies are nothing if not a tangible reminder that we exist in a particular place, and only one place at a time. 'Anatomy is destiny,' wrote Freud, referring to a girl who thought she was a failed boy, though he could have been talking about the modern body that thinks of itself as a failed human. Perhaps the idealisation of space, and the suspicion of place, lurks behind the cult of perfected bodies and the desire to be free of flawed particularities.

What not to say

What has this to do with someone moving? It suggests that when a friend tells you they are off, it is unsettling for profound reasons. The experience exposes some of the ambiguities of contemporary existence. If your immediate thought is that you will miss them, then that is also a reflection on the lonely dislocation of modern life. You may want to wish them well, and join in with the excitement of the opportunities that a new place represents. But deeper down you are sad. They will leave you behind and implicitly underline how you are tied to an old place, perhaps not as free as they can be.

Taking exams

'In examinations those who do not wish to know ask questions of those who cannot tell.' Walter Alexander Raleigh

What might be said

I have a confession to make. I liked exams. I loved the focus they brought to those few weeks of the summer, the tense energy they demanded, the sense that reserves of knowledge were to be put to use, and afterwards the pleasure of something completed. It was my experience of what sports-people describe as 'being in the zone'. I understood the link between learning and happiness.

With that off my chest, let me ask you, dear reader, a question. Are you now reeling with revulsion, thinking that the above paragraph is one of the most perverse confessions that could be made; or do you too understand the mind-stretching joys of the examination?

This is the problem with exams. How do you ask someone who has just been through the Ramadan of the educational year how it went? One person's slow crucifixion is another's crucible of formation. You can observe the difference when students leave the examination room. 'That was awful,' murmur those for whom it was a tribulation. 'That went well,' say those for whom it was a pleasure. 'That was easy,' sneer those who hated it but don't want anyone else to know.

Here's a consolation for those who hate exams, and a challenge to those who love them. Socrates – the founder of Western philosophy, a man whose name is synonymous with intelligence, the wisest person who ever lived, according to Plato, who himself was no dunce – would have thought that exams were worse than a waste of time. Had he been asked about written papers and matriculations he would probably have said that they teach you to leap hurdles, not live life; cram facts, not explore values; stuff information in, not draw insights out.

Having said that, he was no educational libertarian. Like Jesus, who told the rich man that he must give up his wealth in order to gain life, Socrates had a reputation for exacting the highest standards. He cursed the sophists for nurturing a lust for arguments rather than a love of truth; he told more than one precocious Athenian youth that he must develop a skill for honesty not showiness to be smart; and some people described talking with him as like being stung by a ray. If they saw him coming across the agora, they would turn in the opposite direction and disappear into the crowd.

Socrates would not have liked exams, but he loved the toughest personal examination.

What is at stake

John Stuart Mill, the philosopher, had the most extraordinary education. His father's aspirations for his son make today's ambitious parents look as neglectful as the Pentagon's post-invasion planning department. Father had the young Mill studying Greek and arithmetic at three, philosophy and ancient history at six, actively engaging with contemporary books at ten, and making novel contributions to economics and logic at fourteen. He attended university in France and, like the child who recently graduated in maths from Oxford at the age of twelve, Mill achieved some notoriety as a result of his brilliance.

He wrote about it in his *Autobiography*. As soon as it was published it provoked admiration and horror in equal measure. However, he is an interesting person to read on education, not merely for the astonishment provided by his own. He wrote an account of his life precisely to examine what value his education had. The nineteenth-century in which he lived was intensely interested in how people should be taught. It should also be added that he did not regard himself as a prodigy or exception: what happened to him might be a suitable education for anyone.

His father's aim was not only to fill his mind but to shape it, after the manner of the founder of utilitarianism, Jeremy Bentham, whom he adulated. He taught his son himself, and both father and son enjoyed the demanding memory, assessment and exposition exercises. Mill testified that he had a happy childhood and loved the books he devoured.

However, at the age of twenty something changed. Mill had a 'mental crisis', or what we would call a breakdown. He said it was like waking from a happy dream and returning to a grey world in which nothing yields joy. His heart sank; the foundations of his life crumbled. 'I seemed to have nothing left to live for.' He later read these words of Coleridge, which struck him as a true description of his state of mind: 'Work without hope draws nectar in a sieve, And hope without an object cannot live.'

The clouds thickened for some months. He found no comfort in his books. He came to believe that analysing everything, as his education taught him to do, has a tendency to erode feelings. It generates clear-sightedness but dissolves passion; it is unnatural and out of balance. The difficulty was that, although he could analyse his melancholic predicament, he could do nothing about it. The direction of his life, and his character, seemed to be fixed by his learning.

However, a turning point came when his feelings found a channel for their expression, particularly in the poetry of Wordsworth. He read of the power of rural beauty and felt a new sympathy and imagination for the world that had been absent before. Such contemplation suggested a perennial source of delight. Mill could identify with it, but it also, importantly, transcended the limitations of his own training. It drew him out of himself.

Mill wrote that there were two things that he learnt from his crisis. First, that happiness is found incidentally in life: 'Ask yourself whether you are happy, and you cease to be so.' Second, that an education which focuses exclusively on ordering, analysing and speculating is not enough. 'The cultivation of the feelings became one of the cardinal points in my ethical and philosophical creed,' he continued. Poetry, art, music and culture were the best ways to make sense of life, but, Mill warned, one must be careful about how these subjects are taught, let alone examined. An analysis of music, for example, that relentlessly scrutinises how the five tones and two semi-tones of the octave might be put together would rapidly exhaust the pleasure that music can give.

To put it another way, Mill had discovered what is called a liberal education, the approach to learning that is undermined by a so-called vocational education – one that prioritises and orientates itself around qualifications, skills and exams.

What not to say

Mill's mature reflections upon his childhood did not reject the value of being able coolly to analyse things; it was rather a question of balance. Neither do his thoughts easily justify the philosophy that children should be allowed simply to be children – whatever that might mean. He believed his experience proved that much may be taught, 'and well taught, in those early years which, in the common modes of what is called instruction, are little better than wasted'.

However, he had learnt that a formal education, and the exams that go with it, are not everything. At best, it is only half an education, and the less humanising half at that. 'Education is an admirable thing, but it is well to remember from time to time that nothing that is worth knowing can be taught,' wrote Oscar Wilde. Perhaps that is something that can be said to anyone, regardless of their feelings about exams.

Making a complaint

'Take care to get what you like or you will be forced to like what you get.' George Bernard Shaw

What might be said

The world, it is sometimes said, can be divided into two. There are people who love cats, and those who loathe them. There are some who eat Marmite, and some who think it tastes as it looks. There are those who are with us and those who are against us; hawks and doves; sheep and goats; happy people and funny people; those who deploy Microsoft and those who denounce Microsoft. And, of course, there are those who believe that the world can be divided into two, and those who don't.

Well, another divide might be between those who complain and those who would rather wake up from the dream in which they are stripped of their clothes in the park and find it was real, than make a complaint. Those who complain will not hesitate to send back the food, query the bill and leave without tipping. They do it without fear or anxiety. The same situation causes *plangophobes* blind panic. They become flushed, withdraw into a silent flap, and fail to find the right words. This chapter is for them, that they might be empowered to stand up for their rights.

There are, I think, few more frustrating humiliations that modern living forces upon one than having to complain to functionaries who, as cogs in the machine, are powerless to do anything substantial about it. It might be that a flight was delayed, a parcel lost, an allowance late, or that the telephone-line went down. In each case, your dignity and need requires the complaint to be made, and yet you know that the balance is tipped against you. If by chance you do get the right person on the end of the phone, or the right address to write to, you are condemned to appear querulous or imperious, not reasonable or simply right. Whether or not your complaint is acted upon is another question entirely.

Perhaps this is why complaints are a staple of humour. Oscar Wilde once complained to an incapable waiter: 'When I asked for a watercress sandwich, I did not mean a loaf with a field in the middle of it.'

Lord Emsworth, the creation of P. G. Wodehouse, had no one to complain to about the heat of the marquee erected for the August fête: 'Conditions during the tea hour, the marquee having stood all day under a blazing sun, were generally such that Shadrach, Meshach and Abednego, had they been there, could have learned something new about burning fiery furnaces.'

Throwing some wisdom in with the wit, La Rochefoucauld wrote: 'Everyone complains of his memory and no one complains of his judgement.'

I have a friend who is similarly blessed with an ego-preserving quickness of mind. He once told me about being stopped by a policeman for edging over, and only edging over, the speed limit in his car. Stopping him was entirely unnecessary as there was no one else on the road, but the blue lights flashed in his rear-view mirror, he pulled over and wound down the window. The officer cleared his throat and began his speech on the dangers of speeding; everything he said was quite true and utterly patronising.

Most people would sit obediently and listen. My friend didn't – and his opportunity to complain came when the policeman rose to a concluding climax by referring to the adverts currently running on TV that graphically illustrated the dangers of speed.

'Advertisements?' my friend queried in his best posh voice. 'Officer, do I look like the sort of person who watches commercial television?'

He saved his dignity, if not the cash for the fine.

What is at stake

The key to fearless complaining, I suggest, is the cultivation of the right kind of hate. In this, I take a lead from an essay of the nineteenth-century writer, William Hazlitt. It is called 'On the pleasure of hating'.

There is, of course, bad hatred. This is the sort of hate that fuels xenophobia, defeats love, disregards forgiveness, seeks revenge, suffocates the soul and destroys the self. Hazlitt explores some manifestations of negative hatred. It is the self-righteousness that eats into the heart of religion and causes it to sanction bigotry, hypocrisy and heinous crimes. It is the same hatred that poisons national pride and 'makes patriotism an excuse for carrying fire, pestilence and famine into other lands'. The ills of war have not much changed since Victorian times; nor, presumably has the hatred that would perpetrate them.

Another angle on bad hatred is to note that it lacks the facility for self-criticism. It is this kind of hatred that begrudges the abilities of others, cannot share in the success of a friend, and for twisted, ill-defined reasons repays kindness with malignancy. What appears to have happened in such festering spirits is that a hatred which was directed at themselves has been transferred to the world around them. An uncritical hatred is also one that is irresponsible, in the sense that it leads to a habit of blame. Such hate-filled people are never able to admit to their own liability but, like petulant teenagers, are always looking for someone else to accuse.

Finally, Hazlitt says, hatred is unforgivable when it revels in violence and cruelty.

However, there is a hatred that, like anger, can be a positive force. It is good hatred. This is the kind that loathes indulgent calculations about the rights and wrongs of a situation, and leapfrogs equivocation with action. It is hatred that abhors injustice and would fight for something to be done rather than nothing. It also has the virtue of empowering the individual to punch above their weight; it takes away fear. It is the sort of hatred that I heard a woman say she had found when she was attacked in the street: a voice flared up inside her, dispelling the darkness of her fear, yelling, 'For this, I will not stand.'

It is also hatred that can renew your life, since in coming to despise your old opinions or realising the paucity of your previous tastes in books or music, you are propelled towards new things. In this sense, to hate is to be alive. 'Without something to hate, we should lose the very spring of thought and action,' reflects Hazlitt.

Such hatred can be hard to pitch right. For some time, I was in the habit of admitting that there had been one person in my life that I truly hated, namely an old college principal. I thought that he was as scheming and bullying as a Borgia pope, and poisoned a place that might otherwise have been quite happy. From what others said, this judgement was not wholly off the mark, and arguably we saved the college from some of his worst excesses, emboldened by our feelings. But such hatred can easily turn bitter; if it morphs into an internal canker it sours the soul and achieves nothing in terms of the greater good.

Yet, for all its risks, Hazlitt wants to encourage good hatred. He believes it would make the world a better place. His essay rises in pitch to yield a purple passage that is almost a creed:

> Seeing all this as I do, and unravelling the web of human life into its various threads of meanness, spite, cowardice, want of feeling, and want of understanding, of indifference towards others and ignorance of ourselves – seeing custom prevail over all excellence, itself giving away to infamy – mistaken as I have been in my public and private hopes, calculating others from myself, and calculating wrong; always disappointed where I placed most reliance; the dupe of friendship, and the fool of love; have I not reason to hate and to despise myself? Indeed I do; and chiefly for not having hated and despised the world enough.

What not to say

The self-pity that gave Hazlitt good reason to hate and despise himself is the same self-pity of those who routinely hold back from complaining. The danger is twofold. Not complaining can erode self-esteem, and it can excuse injustices, great and small: 'In private life do we not see hypocrisy, servility, selfishness, folly, and impudence succeed, whilst modesty shrinks from the encounter, and merit is trodden under foot?' asks Hazlitt.

But having acknowledged it like that, the new thought – the good hatred – might become a passion that can turn those who hold back. It can motivate a just sentiment that, put to good use, can elicit a complaint.

So start small. Explore the new possibility, the character-building pleasure of hatred. Next time an occasion arises for a simple, justified complaint, refuse to think of it as a threat and seize it as an opportunity. Do not lose your voice, say something. As the saying goes: 'All that is required for evil to triumph is that good men and women do nothing.'

TXT MSG lingo

'On the internet, nobody knows you are a dog.'   Peter Steiner

What might be said

Wen u rx a tx DY evr 1dr w@ it rly means:-)? It is not just a matter of deciphering the codes. To understand a text message, you have to read between the symbols to gauge the mood, or interpret the 'emoticons': is it meant seriously, cynically or as a joke? Knowing who sent the message might help, though friends can easily be misunderstood too. 'Nt 2nite. Iv stuf 2 do.' At least when you were stood up on the phone, you could hear the bugger's tone of voice.

It is better if the text is one of a series, because context is illuminating – which is why it often requires a return text to clarify what has been said. Little wonder that the volume of text messages rises by 300 billion year on year worldwide, and is estimated to reach 2.3 trillion by the end of the decade. One text cascades into others.

If a text can conceal as much as it shows, the same is true of emails. The problem has particularly come to the fore in business, where email libel and slander are major concerns.

A casual email could be in poor taste but, in truth, no worse than the sort of thing that used to be said around the photocopier. Online, it can lead to you defending yourself in court.

There is no doubt that a major attraction of emails is that you can hide behind them. It is easier to lie, to obfuscate, to dismiss, to fake it with electronic communication. This, I am sure, is why video phones have never taken off. Who wants to be seen by the vast majority of people they speak to? When you do not know what to say, you do not want to be seen not saying it!

Professor Ray Pahl, a sociologist and co-author of *Rethinking Friendship: Hidden Solidarities Today*, was asked to carry out some research by BlackBerry. He spoke with a number of the PDA's celebrity users to find out just what role 24/7 email played in their relationships. Unsurprisingly, these people, for whom to work is to network, have wide circles of contacts: on average their 'little black book' bulges with almost 400 people. Yet they could count the number of people they regarded as 'nearest and dearest' on two hands. Even good friends did not number more than a couple of dozen.

The research showed that the greater the size of your social network, the more significance is placed on the value of an inner core of close friends. And the technology enables the celebrities to maintain both. It can be used to keep mere acquaintances at bay, by filtering communications. And it can be used to keep soulmates up close, ensuring that they are available to each other even when physically apart.

So the internet impacts on different kinds of relationships in different ways. For relationships that are really just acquaintanceships or virtual encounters, the effect of online and mobile media is ambivalent; it may as easily lead to tears as trust. But for relationships that people would otherwise robustly refer to as close friendships, these methods of communicating are a positive boon.

What is at stake

Some heralds of the internet age have declared that with virtuality will come almost indefinitely expanding circles of rich, rewarding relationships. Alongside the exponential growth of texts and emails, they point to social websites like MySpace and Second Life.

The reality, though, is less revolutionary – and for a simple reason. Close friendship depends on face-to-face contact, and the meaningful sharing of lives. For all that people find support, solace and simply something to do that involves other people by virtue of being online, such forms of communication are of themselves stunted, humanly speaking. When it comes to fixing meetings or exchanging information this does not usually matter. When it comes to deepening relationships it does. It is just too easy to be misunderstood or deceived. As the student of semiotics might put it, signifiers need the signified to communicate significantly.

Another piece of research found that about 40 per cent of the personal profiles on MySpace were 'economical with the truth' – and, of course, you don't know which 40 per cent. About the only foolproof guard against online guile is when the exchanges can draw on a relationship established in the flesh. Then they are understood.

However, there is perhaps a deeper reason to be concerned about conducting relationships on the internet. It was highlighted by the philosopher Martin Heidegger, and his thoughts on technology. He does not condemn technology like a Luddite, but he does recognise that technology shapes our experience of the world, or 'enframes' it. Technology mediates the world to us, like astronomers who observe a star through the Hubble Space telescope; they do not see the star at all, but a computer-enhanced version of the photons that reach earth from it.

The worry is that, as technology increasingly envelops our world, and our relationships, it increasingly forms them too. This may be behind the fear of those who lament the effect of texts and emails on people's grammar and spelling: grammar and spelling matter because without them it is not possible to communicate richly and well. And all this is a paradox too, of course, since at the same time technology brings us closer together.

A different example of his ambivalence about technology is beautifully explored in Heidegger's account of his journey to Greece in a travelogue entitled *Sojourns*. Greece was not just a tourist destination for him. It was the birthplace of the ancient philosophers who had so inspired him, and so also the cradle of his own thought. However, as he approaches the great places of Delos, Athens and Delphi, he becomes increasing anxious. He realises that the very technology that allows him to travel – technology like his cruise ship – is also an impediment to his experience of the Greece of ancient times.

The problem is that the ship dictates so much of his experience, from the itinerary to the people who accompany him. (He is not very tolerant of tourists, for all that he is one himself, and notes how they 'throw' their experiences into snapshots, their cameras barely allowing them to experience where they are at all.) Anyone who has had the romance of an arrival ruined by having to wait for a late plane in a crowded departure lounge will understand: it does not take much of a delay to wonder whether the journey is worth it. Perhaps technology controls and colours so much of our experience that it effectively obliterates it, Heidegger wonders. He longs for a way of travelling that is not prescribed, but that provides a way that is also a 'being-on-the-way'.

Technology does not quite ruin the trip for Heidegger. When he arrives at Delos his fears subside. The repleteness of the island's abandoned ruins speak across the centuries. The columns sing like the strings of a lyre 'on which perhaps the winds play songs of mourning, inaudible to mortals – echoes of the flight of the gods'. In spite of the technology, and because of it, he senses a meaningful presence.

What not to say

In the less rarefied world of everyday texts and emails, there is evidence that people seek to pierce technology's possible concealments too. They do so by seeking to meet and speak in the flesh.

Consider the town outside Toronto called Netville. It is a modern suburban development that is distinguished by having built-in high-speed internet connectivity. Residents could go online and speak with their neighbours as easily as they can turn on the lights. It might be thought that they would, therefore, stay indoors, not needing the inconvenience of stepping outside and walking across the road, but the opposite was found to be the case. These neighbours were more likely to meet each other face-to-face than most; the technology became a bridge not a barrier.

So the next time you receive a text that is as obscure as the Da Vinci code, don't reply, 'W@?' Try instead, 'We shd mEt F2F.'

Going green

'The greater the wealth, the thicker will be the dirt.'

J. K. Galbraith, author of *The Affluent Society*

What might be said

In 1982, Mrs Thatcher, the British Prime Minister, made a speech to her party conference. It was the time of the Falklands War, the conflict that made her. She told the adoring crowd: 'It is exciting to have a real crisis on your hands, when you have spent half your political life dealing with humdrum issues like the environment.'

In just a few short years, such a sentiment has become unthinkable – let alone uttered with such glee. War continues to excite politicians: like the poor, it is always with us. However, few would have guessed that by the turn of the century the environment would have become such a burning issue.

Now, political leaders find they are forced to defend extraneous flights not absolutely vital for the job. If they want to set an example, they travel on scheduled flights, not specially chartered planes, as they might have done before without thinking twice. You have to have sympathy for them. Surely these are just the first salvoes in the barrage of shots that will be fired at leaders who claim to be setting an environmental agenda one week, before stepping onto a jet plane the next.

The political will become increasingly personal too, in the sense that we will all find ourselves more open to charges of climate change hypocrisy or selfish carbon indulgence. Already, the bottom has fallen out of the 'Chelsea tractor' market in the UK; these 4x4 vehicles now carry too much stigma. The practice of carbon off-setting is just about justifying the behaviour of those who feel guilty about taking city-breaks and cheap flights. You may have switched your light bulbs to low energy, installed a mini-windmill on the roof, and switched to a hybrid car. But still your eco-warrior friends, who donate enough cash to plant a small forest every time they heat their soup, chastise you for having a bunker-busting carbon footprint. You are caught on the horns of an apocalyptic dilemma.

There is an ancient myth retold by Plato. Phaethon, a young boy, bragged to his friends that his father was the god of the Sun, Helios. They did not believe him, so the boy made his father promise him anything he wanted.

Phaethon requested a day driving his father's chariot, the sun, across the heavens. Helios could not talk him out of it, and when Phaethon took the reigns, he lost control of the white horses, incinerated every plant and living thing on the earth's surface, and was himself killed by a thunderbolt.

Plato remembered this story of environmental catastrophe as an example of the kind of monumental event that changes everything.

After it, the people of the earth could not recall how they lived before. They lost touch with their history, traditions and way of life.

Could climate change do the same for our children after this century? Might future generations remember the greenhouse disaster as a kind of Noah's flood – a purge of individualistic degeneracy and materialistic excess?

What is at stake

Peter Singer is an impressive philosopher because his thoughts have achieved that rare thing: they have discernibly changed the world. In an age in which most of his academic colleagues are engaged in a careful process of dotting analytical 'i's and crossing clarificatory 't's, his book *Animal Liberation* fired a campaign and movement. If all decent people should seek to minimise suffering, why is it that we turn a blind eye to the suffering we mete out on animals, he asked? His answer is that in the vast majority of cases we discriminate against them because they are not members of the human species. So whilst there might be good reasons for keeping animals humanely for food, or experimenting on them for medical advances, 'speciesism' alone is not justification enough.

The response we make to climate change is an ethical decision of equal complexity and proportion because, as with animals, our use and abuse of the environment is integral to our daily lives. If Singer brought clarity to our treatment of animals, can his philosophy do the same when it comes to the question of going green?

His approach is utilitarian, which is to say that he thinks ethics is a matter of making arguments that by the force of their reason alone become irresistible. In general, he believes that we should not just act in our own self-interest because it is clear that the interests of others around us need to be taken into account too. This, in turn, means that we should think of the effects of our actions on the society in which we live; and, widening the circle of our considerations again, that we should bear in mind the interests of human beings as a whole.

When it comes to climate change, Singer does not believe that it is worth trying to make arguments about the environment's intrinsic value stand up, as many in the green movement would want to do. He says that only sentient beings have such worth, and what ever the biosphere might be, it does not feel or perceive its 'suffering' as a result of greenhouse gases. Rather, he argues that damage to the environment has such a catastrophic impact on the lives of our fellow humans and other species that individuals and governments should make drastic changes to the way we live in order to protect it.

In another of his best-selling books, *How Are We to Live?*, he shows that this approach is radically different from the free-market economics of Adam Smith. In Smith's day, it was possible to argue that in absolute terms the rich consume little more than the poor, even if the rich are selfish and rapacious: there are plenty of the necessities of life to go around. But, continues Singer, Smith's argument has ceased to apply.

Smith never dreamt that the capacity of the atmosphere to absorb pollutants might be a finite resource. So while he knew that the rich could be selfish and rapacious, he did not image that they could take six times their share of the global atmospheric sink. Far from dividing the produce of all their improvements with the poor, the rich are presently on course to drown tens of millions of poor people who have the misfortune to live in low-lying coastal areas, and to starve untold millions more, as climate change makes the lands on which they depend increasingly arid.

This is what he calls a good ethical argument; and it is forceful. Having said that, Singer is a realist too. He knows that not everyone, or even most people, will be persuaded to change. 'There will always be people who don't care for anyone or anything, not even for themselves,' he coolly continues: 'There will be others, more numerous and more calculating, who earn a living by taking advantage of others, especially the poor and the powerless.'

His hope, though, is that enough will. They will cultivate a 'higher ethical consciousness' that can stand against the selfish rich. By radically rethinking their goals – the most fundamental questions about how they live – they will create new priorities that in time other people may come to emulate. These people too might then realise that a life of pure consumption, regardless of its impact upon others, is not the happiest life possible. Rather, the best way of life is one that is ethical.

What not to say

There is no easy answer to this. Singer talks about the evidence, about the drowning and starving millions. The question is whether even such unforgiving facts and figures can inspire personal change, not least when many are genuinely unsure of just what change is necessary?

For one thing, it is not at all clear that the efforts of a single individual can make much difference. The thriftiest person in the West inevitably does more than their fair share of damage just by living in the West. We may feel better for going green – as global economic forces continue to charge the atmosphere with toxins. But so what?

Also, many people will fight back in response to so gloomy a vision. One of the problems of the environmental movement is, paradoxically, the fact that its ethics is premised on the pain and suffering of millions. The trouble with being haunted by such a spectre is that, in practice, it is as likely to provoke antagonism against its aims as sympathy for them. Like the serpent in Eden, it nurtures a blame culture – as when high-profile figures are singled out for particular criticism. And it can overwhelm individuals with its fatalism; the old nostrum of seizing the day can become a scorched-earth policy, through the bleak logic that tomorrow we will burn.

The fact that it is so hard to imagine what it might be like to readjust our priorities and still live well, without such high levels of consumption, is one reason why the present situation is so depressing. Plato's myth may one day not seem so ancient.

Compromising decisions

'Waste no more time arguing what a good man should be. Be one.'

Marcus Aurelius

What might be said

Think of the different moral connotations associated with these two statements:

1. We'll find a compromise.
2. You are compromised.

The first, an intention, would generally be thought morally good. On the whole, people would say that to find a compromise on some matter is to seek a virtuous route through a complex issue. It entails learning to live with your neighbour, respecting difference, and exercising personal humility rather than haughtiness.

The second sounds very different. It is a condemnation. To say that someone is compromised is to suggest that they do not have principles, that they are corrupt, servile or shameless, that they are not their own person. Compromising individuals demean themselves with a vice.

So how can it be that the person who seeks compromise is saluted, whilst the individual who is compromised is spurned? How can so much turn on such an apparently subtle difference? And might you yourself be compromised if, unwittingly, you fail to distinguish between the two in some decision you take?

There are some cases when to be compromised is clearly to be at fault. There is one test that is invariably illuminating: did the compromise have a price? When money exchanges hands, someone has been bought. As Tennyson observed: 'The jingling of the guinea helps the hurt that Honour feels.'

Often, however, the morality of compromise is far from clear cut. In 2007, an argument about compromise raged in British politics, consuming column inches in the press, and apparently causing the Prime Minister sleepless nights. The issue at stake was whether Catholic adoption agencies should be allowed to refuse homosexual couples solely on the basis that they are gay. To the Catholics, the issue is straightforward: homosexual practice is wrong and so they should be allowed an exception in equality law – a compromise that would permit them to say no and refer such couples to other agencies. To the proponents of gay equality, that is a compromise too far: if you allow an exception in one case you must allow exceptions in others and the universality of equality law is undermined.

Personally, I side with gay equality. The adoption of a child should be decided in the best interests of the child, so automatically ruling out a group of people who might provide good homes is to act in the interests of a prior ideology rather than the child. However, the Catholics had a more subtle argument too. In a plural society not everyone will have the same view on moral matters, so to prevent a democracy becoming a tyranny of the majority, compromises must be made. In principle, if not over this particular issue, I can see the necessity of that.

What is at stake

Marcus Tullius Cicero lived in one of the most turbulent periods in political history, the dying days of the Roman Republic. Publicly, he spoke uncompromisingly in favour of Republican values. Privately, Cicero knew that the success of the Republic was itself a product of endless compromises between different power brokers and so he had to be adept at compromise too. In this, he differed from his contemporary Marcus Porcius Cato, whose name was a byword for uncompromising standards but who, because he was so immovable, was still led to immoral actions – or so Cicero argued.

Cicero's compromises worked. They carried him to the pinnacle of Roman society when he was elected consul in 63 BCE. His work *On Duties*, written later, in the last year of his life, is his reflection on how to live up to the highest possible moral standards given the often slippery ethics of the greasy pole. Book III is subtitled 'The Conflict Between the Right and the Expedient'. In it, he debates whether it is always wrong to kill, to break promises, to seek pleasure. The short answer is no: all rules have exceptions. So he seeks not to establish absolute moral laws, but to identify guiding principles that, if followed, will steer his readers towards good compromises and away from bad ones.

The immediate compromise that Cicero finds himself making, as he writes, is being away from Rome. (At the time, he judged it too dangerous a place for him to be, which caused him anxiety as he felt it was his duty to contribute to political life.) This is a compromise that might also suggest cowardice, so he highlights a first principle: when faced with a choice of evils, one ought not only to choose the least evil but also exploit any good elements that it may contain. His self-imposed political absence, then, he will put to good use by writing *On Duties*.

A number of principles emerge:

- Always have a moral argument for what you do, even if it is not watertight. This is about your direction of travel: if you turn your back on what might be right, in favour of what is merely expedient, you are looking the wrong way and may never recover your moral orientation.

- Do not conceal your moral compromises, especially when they are real and unavoidable. Pretence and deceit – spinning, we might add – always produce ills of their own. To put it another way: act in good faith. 'The morally wrong cannot by any possibility be made morally right, however successfully it may be covered up,' Cicero aphorises. Also, this attitude is one that best allows people to learn from moral mistakes.

- Try to be consistent. For example, it is absurd to say, as Cicero observes some people do, that they would never rob a parent or friend, when they would think nothing of essentially doing just that in relation to the rest of humanity. Consistency is also important because without it moral argument becomes self-serving sophistry, and can lead to the creation of monsters who can justify anything.

- Don't injure others for your own gain. Cicero recalls something the stoic philosopher Chrysippus said. When athletes take part in a race, it is their duty to do everything they can to win, so long as that does not involve tripping up their fellow competitors. Chrysippus concludes: 'Thus, in the stadium of life, it is not unfair for anyone to seek to obtain what is needful for his own advantage, but he has no right to wrest it from his neighbour.'

- On a related point, cruelty is always wrong. Cicero remembers the Athenians who cut off the thumbs of the Aeginetans. Thus mutilated, they would never again be able to sail to Piraeus and threaten the city. However, Cicero thinks this was an abhorrent act for all that it was expedient.

- If a compromise involves self-sacrifice it is likely to be one that is morally good. For self-sacrifice is an indication of someone's good character; they prefer the life of service to that of pleasure.

- Make the most of your talents. If you are given much, in terms of education, power, wealth or responsibility, then you should exercise these to the best of your ability. Sins of omission are as grave as sins of commission.

- Seek harmony, not discord. Ideally, the interests of the individual will coincide with the interests of the body politic as a whole. But if that is not absolutely attainable, then moves in the direction of such harmony will be better than moves towards discord.

- Always honour good friendship, and be wary of

friendships that are really conspiracies. 'Apparent advantages – political preferment, riches, sensual pleasures, and the like – should never be preferred to the obligations of friendship,' Cicero writes. He knew this from his own experience, having recently suffered from the betrayal of his sometime friend Marc Antony.

Throughout these guiding principles, Cicero highlights a common thread: moral goodness and practical expediency must ultimately not be at odds with one another, but must coincide. It may often be hard to see how, but the hope should not be abandoned. For to give up on that is to make morality purely relative, or to justify an immoral means by supposed moral ends: 'To this error the assassin's dagger, the poisoned cup, the forged wills owe their origin; this gives rise to theft, embezzlement of public funds, exploitation and plundering of provincials and citizens; this engenders also the lust for excessive wealth, for despotic power, and finally for making oneself king even in the midst of a free people; and anything more atrocious or repulsive than such a passion cannot be conceived.'

What not to say

If is, of course, possible to quibble with Cicero over the details. However, he is on the right track in terms of negotiating the twists and turns of practical ethics. There is perhaps one imperative that sums up his approach, and that is the search for integrity.

Integrity is a quality that is above moral rules, though there could be no such thing as immoral integrity.

Conversely, merely to obey laws, as if that were the sum total of morality, would be slavish rather than moral. Integrity is a question of character, and the principles that Cicero distils come directly from his struggle to develop his character.

Someone who acts with integrity is always worthy of respect, if not agreement. And although integrity is itself a virtue that should be scrutinised – for the principles it makes manifest in practice – more often than not it is intuitively possible to discern its presence, or absence, in what people say and do.

So the difference between 'finding a compromise' and 'being compromised' rests on acting with integrity. This is the test, and can determine what you say about someone's need to compromise, or not.

Talking politics

'War is nothing but a continuation of politics with the admixture of other means.'   Karl von Clausewitz

What might be said

To talk politics, it might be said, is to achieve one of two things. It either seals friendship, or it confirms enemies. Thus, to avoid talking politics is almost a natural instinct, amicable human interactions being at least partly a question of maintaining agreement. Only when we can be sure that our interlocutors share our viewpoint can we safely venture onto political terrain.

'In politics the middle way is none at all,' mused John Adams, the second President of the US. 'We have no eternal allies and we have no perpetual enemies. Our interests are eternal,' declared Lord Palmerston, the nineteenth-century British Prime Minister. 'There are no true friends in politics. We are all sharks circling, and waiting, for traces of blood to appear in the water,' wrote the diarist and politician Alan Clark.

The message seems clear: don't talk politics.

At university, the Student Union always intimidated me. I was quite heavily involved, being a Welfare Affairs officer in my second year. With a cup of coffee and a packet of ten cigarettes, I could often be found sitting in the Union cafeteria. Friends would join me to idle away the hours between and through lectures.

Being a flâneur was easy. Being an activist was not. The trouble was that I didn't have an ideology (I was prime electoral material for Tony Blair in 1997). The body of activists I might most naturally have gravitated towards were the Liberal Democrats, but they were unappealingly, flagrantly bourgeois. The Marxists offered me another choice, but they couldn't offer me a political home because *I* was unappealingly, flagrantly bourgeois. And in any case, I couldn't grasp the distinction between the Trotskyites, Maoists and Leninists sufficiently to hurl leftist insults with ease. There was a solitary Tory in the Union, who is now an MP. Everyone loathed him of course, it being the Thatcher years, though at least his convictions lent him self-respect.

What is at stake

However, it is also said that politics is too serious a matter to be left to the politicians. And, in fact, this is right. Plato, for one, argues why in his dialogue about an idealised city-state, the *Republic*.

There is much that reads uncomfortably in Plato from the viewpoint of a modern, liberal democracy. He argues that parents should not be allowed to raise children themselves, but that they should be brought up collectively, in the community. It is also fashionable amongst commentators to highlight Plato's failure when he attempted to practise what he preached. He reluctantly tried to reform the dictator of Syracuse, Dionysius II, and when he failed to do so, turned to that old political excuse of saying that events didn't allow him enough time.

However, there is one insight that Plato puts at the start of the *Republic* that is certainly worth considering. It might be summarised thus: politics is nothing if it does not nurture civic friendship.

The thought appears in the first section of the *Republic*, during a discussion of justice. One of the participants, Thrasymachus, asks Socrates whether justice pays – which is to say that he is equally prepared to act unjustly when that brings him rewards. Socrates dismisses that as the 'justice' of dictators. His point is that society cannot flourish for its citizens under a system of arbitrary justice. It needs citizens and rulers who are truly just.

This is partly for the reason that the law is an ass when it comes to so much of human affairs. It cannot mediate on most of the things that matter in life: a society functions far better when most people, most of the time, themselves act fairly in their daily lives. This much any modern democrat would concur with, hence the fact that words like 'decency' and 'tolerance' routinely feature in political discourse.

However, Plato has a more profound issue in mind too, one that is commonly, perhaps even deliberately, sidelined today. For justice is but an abstract expression of a greater connection between citizens in the ideal city; that connection is civic friendship.

Civic friendship is the implicit sense of care and concern that citizens have for one another. It begins with the personal friendships that people share and, by analogy, extends out, in ripples of affection, to embrace all those with whom you are politically connected. It means that you not only agree to cooperate with others, as the appeal to justice, decency and tolerance implies. Further, it means that you positively wish them well. After all, Plato writes later in the *Republic*, 'Friends share all things in common' – rehearsing an Athenian commonplace that was quoted almost as frequently in ancient political philosophy as the modern truism, 'All people love freedom.'

Friendship, as opposed to justice, matters because of who we are as humans. As Aristotle was later to abbreviate it: we are political animals. It is not possible to be human apart from society. Or to put it more strongly, it is not possible to be an individual apart from society, since it is a society – with its traditions and culture – that gives us the essentials of what it is to be an individual, from language to a sense of belonging.

Friendship matters to politics in another way too. It is virtues like care and concern that flourish most readily between friends, that are of such value among citizens. So people who are good at friendship are likely to be good at citizenship too. Perhaps it is important to stress that Plato's conception of friendship was neither sentimental, as in Marc Antony's famous Shakespearean 'Friends, Romans, countrymen'; nor was it calculating, as in 'how to win friends and influence people'. Rather, friends should debate and disagree, whilst offering each other respect, and Plato wrote dialogues in which his characters do precisely that. It is only friends, he wrote, who can be genuinely honest with one another and prepared to admit to their faults – more virtues that serve politics well.

This brings us back to the reason why talking about politics is so important. At one level, democracy cannot function without it, which is why it is too important to leave to politicians. And at another level – a more important one – the creation of a society within which individuals can thrive as human beings needs it too, for it is the foundation of civic friendship.

What not to say

There are obvious, extreme cases of what happens when people do not talk politics. Dictators and totalitarian states forbid citizens to do so because if they did dissension would be fomented in the friendships that would form, and injustices would become plain for all to see.

Civil war is again horribly symptomatic of what happens when citizens can no longer converse about the shape of their society. Hence 'to jaw-jaw' is the best antidote to 'war-war'.

But there are more insidious political failures of the good society that reveal themselves in the collapse of civic friendship. Take the so-called surveillance society. Not only does it potentially breed distrust, since the omnipresence of cameras suggests the omnipresence of criminals. It also fosters an approach to politics in which citizens are treated as potential or actual enemies, not friends.

One sign of this is when the role of politicians is perceived as being largely bureaucratic: all their effort goes on managing real or imagined conflicts between citizens. Another is when politicians rarely discuss vision or values, for fear that this might offend people in their pluralistic constituencies. Instead, the rhetoric consists of discussing demands that need to be balanced, like rights and responsibilities. If that sounds a bit contractual, that is because it is – and it does not make for civic friendship.

The remedy is at once simple and challenging: discussion. So talk politics – and talk as actual or would-be friends.

Finding religion

'We have just enough religion to make us hate, but not enough to make us love one another.'. Jonathan Swift

What might be said

The first dinner-party I attended on my first trip to the US swept away my English habit of careful circumlocutions before the first course was finished. I was in New Jersey, on a summer camp, to help teach music to kids whose schools could not provide extra-curricular subjects. The camps were run by an Anglican church and, as I was an ordinand in the Church of England, people at Grace Church, Plainfield were generous with their evening invitations. This one was high-powered, hosted by a wealthy lady (I recall that even her garage had air-conditioning). She had gathered half a dozen of her professional friends to meet me.

But unlike in the UK, where my status as a wannabe priest would have been sidelined as if to say, 'We wouldn't be so rude as to suggest that your personal vocation was a matter for public discussion', in the US it was the very reason to talk.

I was nervous. My middle-class table training warned me that, like politics and sex, religion was a prandial taboo: it was as indigestible as Brussels sprouts or doughy bread. The subject had come up too soon in the evening for me to assess what relationship these folk had with the Almighty. Maybe they were evangelical, in which case it would be wise to steer clear of certain moral issues. Perhaps they were ecclesiastical conservatives and not in favour of women priests, and the conversation would have to be managed so as to avoid subjects that might give them an opportunity for misogyny. They could be atheistically inclined, only maintaining their association with the church like a couple whose marriage has long since failed but who stay together because they are so in love with their anger.

And yet there it was, the very first question: 'Do you think that the Church of England will tear itself apart?' I was trapped quite as squarely as the Pharisees cornered Jesus. If I said yes, I would paint myself as a schismatic. With no, I might appear indifferent to the rightness of the causes involved. Don't know – as just another one of those woolly liberals who are ruining the Mother Church. 'Ah,' I ventured, with faux gravitas, buying time.

Grace is the frankly graceless mother of Tom, a charming student-lawyer, and husband of humane and humorous Tony. Completing the quartet is the quietly strong Ruth, Tom's girlfriend. Grace is a scientist and a famous, proselytising atheist – or rather naturalist, she insists, since atheist is a theological word and so only advertises 'their' dangerous beliefs and infantile superstitions.

Tom, it turns out, is a Christian, not by virtue of any blinding light but by a steady sense that God is a question he cannot put down. Moreover, he wants to pursue his conviction by becoming a priest. Grace is rabidly furious.

This is the scenario laid out in the play *On Religion* by Mick Gordon and A. C. Grayling. It makes for intense intellectual struggle and raw emotion on the matters of science and religion as mother and son refuse to back down. Mealtimes are not easy times in this household.

But who stands out as the person with the most humanity? Not Grace, with her rational integrity to keep intact. Nor Tom, for all that he strives after a higher love. Rather it is Ruth, who is a sort of failed believer. She advocates kindness as a moral excellence – superior to love and reason, for all that love and reason can drive you to fulfilment, or destruction. Why? Because kindness allows others to be. It is closer to compassion than passion. It embodies selflessness.

What is at stake

The trouble with religion is that, at least in theory, it is an all-encompassing world view. It defines your tribe, and fences your community. As the sociologist Emile Durkheim described it, 'God is society, writ large', which means that religion is not only an expression of social cohesion but a calling to put the interests of the populace ahead of your own desires and opinions. This is why it is commonly thought to admit no rivals, and to be the cause of wars. When you have 'seen the light', you never see the world in the same way again – like an Archimedian eureka-moment. You have been converted, and your relationship to the world is premised on the goal of converting others too.

The fear is that 'discussing religion' is as oxymoronic as 'teaching fools' or 'questioning certainty'. Fools are not mindless if they can be taught. Certainty is not unshakeable if it can be questioned. So religion is not about reason and debate, but faith – a breastplate against attack, as the Bible puts it.

Another reason that people hesitate to talk about religion is that it is perceived as a personal matter. To make fun of someone's beliefs – even accidentally – seems as unforgivable as laughing at their child. Religion is, like children, a source of comfort – perhaps the last bastion of hope in an otherwise imploding world. Who could be so callous as to take that comfort away, as long as they keep their beliefs to themselves? 'If it works for them . . .', someone else might venture.

What is going on here can also be understood in the context of the history of religion. It used to be the case that religion was not primarily a personal matter but was one of weighty public and political importance. Wars were indeed fought over it, and people died in hideous ways. However, after the Restoration in England, and at similar moments in the history of other Western countries, laws of toleration were passed that allowed people to worship in the different ways they saw fit. This had the effect of weakening the role that religion could play in public life; it was the beginning of the secular separation of Church and state. To put it another way, religion became a private matter of personal conscience.

Today when people express the same sentiment – that religion should be a private matter – they are echoing an old fear. If believers are forced to defend their religion in public, will the debate not become violent – around the dinner-table as surely as on the international stage?

Conversely, a sceptic might argue that religion is not worth talking about as it is based upon pure superstition. This view says that Christianity or Islam are no more sophisticated than slaughtering goats to Jove or setting up idols to Artemis. In fact, they might add, it is worse since at least these practices had meaning in their time. Religion today comes after the Enlightenment, when rational people discarded inherited belief and thought for themselves. Submitting to a divinity now is as well-founded as worshipping a garden gnome. The existence of a divinity is as likely as a china teapot orbiting the sun between earth and Mars – possible but hardly probable, as Bertrand Russell argued.

From that position it is only a short step to outright hostility towards religion, which suggests another reason for counselling that religion should be approached with caution. It is not only the religious who might resist reasonable discussion. The atheistic might ruin the evening too.

What not to say

On the face of it, the Danish philosopher Søren Kierkegaard is an unlikely figure to rescue us from this predicament. He abandoned his early vocation to become a clergyman and instead took to stigmatising what he saw as the hypocrisy of the Christians of Copenhagen. This reached a climax in 1854, upon the death of Bishop Mynster, the primate of the Church of Denmark. Kierkegaard was furious when the prelate was declared a 'witness to the truth'. Through articles in the press, he launched a furious attack on the clerical establishment that stopped only with his death.

So I am not suggesting that dinner-party discussions about religion would be eased if only Kierkegaard were present. Far from it. However, his plea – no, shout – is helpful, *in absentia*, because it calls everything anyone says about religion into question.

What fired Kierkegaard's antagonism was not a loathing of religion. Rather, it was the widespread misunderstandings about religion that he argued both believers and non-believers have. What they don't understand is that faith is literally impossible. The figure of Abraham is his exemplar in this because it was Abraham who alone passed the great test of faith, namely being prepared to sacrifice his son Isaac. If this seems a horrific thing for a divinity to demand of a father, than that is the point. Faith is as unthinkable as child sacrifice.

Kierkegaard was another failed Christian: he struggled with the deepest challenges that lie behind belief. This struggle became a prophetic voice that mocked those believers who treat religion as a personal source of comfort. Jesus said faith could turn water into wine, he recalls at one point in his book *Fear and Trembling*; these believers would turn wine into water!

And he also mocks those atheists who demand that God be proven by experiment, as if God's existence could be proven, or was even theoretically provable. That 'deity' would not be divine. For first and last, God is transcendent. It is not believers but atheists who have mistaken God for a teapot. They deserve pity not a pat on the back.

What both may close their eyes to is the great challenge

that religion represents to humanity: to move out of the domains of knowledge in which we can be sure and confident, and pursue what lies at the limits of our understanding.

In a way, then, we should practise what Kierkegaard preached about religion – being bold and not afraid. Believers shouldn't be offended, because God can't be offended. Non-believers should be less scornful, for in merely mocking faith, they mock their own humanity that could aspire to transcendence. So make sure you are speaking about religion, not some conception of God that does not deserve the name.

In retrospect, my new American friends had it about right that night. Respectfully, they posed a question. There is hardly anything more important to talk about.

Someone died

'A time to weep, and a time to laugh; a time to mourn, and a time to dance.' Ecclesiastes

What can be said

People are more terrified of saying the wrong thing when faced with a death than perhaps at any other time. The worst is an untimely death – that of, say, a young mother or child. Its utter finality feels horribly disabling. The hopeful word seems cruel, a practical suggestion irrelevant. Like trying to wring water from a dry sponge, words do not flow.

Typically, people adopt one of two strategies. If the death was untimely, they reach for cliché. 'I am so sorry for your loss,' is one formula. It seems inadequate, almost an admission of not knowing what to say, but at least it expresses a sentiment of sympathy.

If the death was half expected, perhaps because the person was old, it is easier to find more to say, such as something pleasant about the deceased. This works fine if the person concerned was likeable, but death releases all sorts of feelings in the minds of the nearest and dearest left behind. If someone was actually an ogre in life, now could be the moment when years of hurt spill out. Even if someone was lovely, the next of kin can have all sorts of bizarre reactions to their death. They can deny that it has happened at all. They might rage at being left alone. They can feel guilty, because when someone else dies this underlines the fact that they themselves live on. A common response to a close death is to feel immortal or triumphant – an ugly thought, from which comes guilt when it is your beloved who has gone the way of all flesh.

Here's a story from when I was a priest. It was a miserable day for a funeral. Steady rain had been falling from grey skies since the sullen dawn, but that was not what was bothering the undertaker. The funeral was a burial, and the downpour was filling up the grave. Now, as the service came to an end, and we prepared to process into the graveyard, I could see him nervously pacing at the back of the church. As I walked past, he whispered, 'It's a lake.' Sure enough, the hole – as precisely angled as an archaeologist's trench – was full of brown, choppy water.

Dead bodies do not take well to waiting. The coffin impacted the surface with a muted thwack. I expected it to sink – perhaps even to look quite dignified. But it didn't. It floated, jerkily rocking.

I began to panic. There are only so many 'comfortable words' in the prayer book. What should I say? I cast an eye across the mourners to gauge their mood.

But unbeknownst to us, at least at first, the coffin had started to fill with water. And just as contingencies were forming in my mind, the air/water ratio reached a tipping point. The coffin lost its buoyancy and sank – emitting the sound of a fart.

> It must have been the work of one of those cheeky, baroque angels. The grandkids started to giggle, and did I really hear someone mutter, 'She's saying goodbye'?

What is at stake

The irony with the struggle to say the right thing at times of death is that it usually does not matter much what you say. Anything will do.

Let me explain. When I was a priest, I took about two funerals a week. Each death required seeing the family on two separate occasions: the first visit to sort out details of the service; the second for the service itself. This meant that, on average, I was with people who were mourning at least every other working day.

When I explained this to friends they were shocked. They assumed that Sunday was the busy day for clergy. 'What on earth do you find to say to all these bereaved people?' they stammered. The short answer is 'not much'. Not because I didn't care – quite the opposite. Nor because there are not all sorts of things that could be said. I did not say much because, at times of death, it is the bereaved who need to speak, in the ways they want to. What you say, as a priest or concerned friend, is only a trigger for them to talk.

After all, though we may miss the person who has died, we do not face the body-blow, the psychic fissure, faced by someone who has lost their other half or their child.

The philosopher Michel de Montaigne, a man who is

sometimes called the French Socrates, provided an insight into just what is at stake for the person who is left. He wrote an essay after a friend died – not just any friend, but a friend who was so close to him that he called him his other self.

> In the friendship that I am talking about, souls are mingled and confounded in so universal a blending that they efface the seam which joins them together so that it cannot be found. If you press me to say why I loved him, I feel that it cannot be expressed except by replying: 'Because it was him: because it was me.' Mediating this union there was, beyond all my reasoning, beyond all that I can say specifically about it, some inexplicable force of destiny.

For Montaigne, his habit of writing essays was the trigger for articulating his loss. And whilst he finds it hard to describe the love that he knew, he does find words to say what that loss is like.

> Since that day when I lost him, I merely drag wearily on. The very pleasures which are proffered me do not console me: they redouble my sorrow at his loss. In everything we were halves: I feel I am stealing his share from him. Nor is it right for me to enjoy pleasures, I decided, while he who shared things with me is absent from me. I was already used and accustomed to being, in everything, one of two, that I now feel I am no more than a half. There is no deed nor thought in which I do not miss him.

This is what we should remember when thinking what to say: we cannot say what needs to be said. Only they can, in their way. And although to hear it is almost unbearable, the great gift we can give to someone who is mourning is to allow them to speak. It is the first step, not to closure, but to learning to live on with the loss.

What not to say

Death is not nice. It is painful, if not bloody. To try to say something as if the right words would magic that away is to be deluded. The only comfort is that it is not what you say that counts – the chances are that it won't be remembered anyway.

The aim is not to say the right thing, it is just to say something, so that the person you are with can talk. Do not speak too much. Say something simple, and then be prepared to listen. But don't say nothing – the bereft must speak in order to mourn.

A Good Death

The deaths that have so far been closest to me, that of my mother and her mother, suggest a further reflection. My grandmother died at the fine age of ninety-four. She was only out of her home for the last two weeks of her life and was miserable then. In the last days she sank fast, and I suspect found great relief in being able to shed life, as opposed to having it cling to her. Her funeral was a wonderful day. Folk from her village filled the pews and we, as family members, were able to contribute our presence, a eulogy, music, readings and even a sermon.

My mother's death was untimely, the grizzly climax of a runaway cancer. For about two years we had lived the roller-coaster lives of those with loved ones nursing malignant tumours. Once I talked to my mother about how it was a kind of gift wrapped in thorns: the illness intensified life and love, and was a kind of blessing. That was an upbeat day. On bad days, everything was brutal and bleak. I recall another visit when my mother sat rocking in her chair, hugging herself. I worried that she would die in such a lacerated state but, actually, I needn't have. For in the last month, when the disease clearly entered its final stage, she developed a profound calmness. It was as if she embraced mortality. She became a little detached, though careful to make sure that we all, individually, shared a loving goodbye. Again, it must have been a relief that her suffering was ending, but she seemed reconciled to the corollary of that: she was ending too.

I would, therefore, say that both my mother and grandmother had a good death. The concept of a good death is one that runs across philosophical and theological traditions. It falls somewhere between the assertion that death is nothing, or nothingness – which to me is as contradictory as saying that the edge of a picture does not frame it – and the assertion that death is just the start of a new life. This appears unfounded since there is only one certainty about death, namely that it is real and will come. A good death embraces the tough terrain of the middle ground. It admits death's weight and is able to carry it. It acknowledges death's fearfulness and finds a way to befriend it.

A good death, therefore, takes time. A sudden death may not actually be a good one because it is like the flip of a coin: whether the person dying and those left are prepared for it is determined by chance. It cuts short the agony, but it cuts short love too. So the old litany prayed: 'Save us from sudden death.' 'To philosophise is to learn how to die,' Montaigne, Cicero and Plato thought. Paradoxically, we must contemplate death in order to learn how to live. Living desperately makes death a terrible struggle. Mortals must pass through death's shadow into the light of life.

It is for this reason that a good death is an achievement. It is one, I believe, that both my grandmother and mother made. For this reason, we who watched their deaths have been thankful again. For the last thing they taught us is how to die and die well.

Index